Policing Dissent

Critical Issues in Crime and Society
Raymond J. Michalowski, Series Editor

Critical Issues in Crime and Society is oriented toward critical analysis of contemporary problems in crime and justice. The series is open to a broad range of topics including specific types of crime, wrongful behavior by economically or politically powerful actors, controversies over justice system practices, and issues related to the intersection of identity, crime, and justice. It is committed to offering thoughtful works that will be accessible to scholars and professional criminologists, general readers, and students.

Tammy L. Anderson, ed., *Neither Villain Nor Victim: Empowerment and Agency among Women Substance Abusers*

Luis A. Fernandez, *Policing Dissent: Social Control and the Anti-Globalization Movement*

Mary Bosworth and Jeanne Flavin, eds., *Race, Gender, and Punishment: From Colonialism to the War on Terror*

Michael J. Lynch, *Big Prisons, Big Dreams: Crime and the Failure of America's Penal System*

Raymond J. Michalowski and Ronald C. Kramer, eds., *State-Corporate Crime: Wrongdoing at the Intersection of Business and Government*

Susan L. Miller, *Victims as Offenders: The Paradox of Women's Violence in Relationships*

Susan F. Sharp, *Hidden Victims: The Effects of the Death Penalty on Families of the Accused*

Robert H. Tillman and Michael L. Indergaard, *Pump and Dump: The Rancid Rules of the New Economy*

Mariana Valverde, *Law and Order: Images, Meanings, Myths*

Michael Welch, *Scapegoats of September 11th: Hate Crimes and State Crimes in the War on Terror*

Policing Dissent

SOCIAL CONTROL AND THE ANTI-GLOBALIZATION MOVEMENT

LUIS A. FERNANDEZ

RUTGERS UNIVERSITY PRESS
New Brunswick, New Jersey, and London

Library of Congress Cataloging-in-Publication Data

Fernandez, Luis A., 1969–
   Policing dissent : social control and the anti-globalization move-
ment / Luis A. Fernandez.
      p.   cm. – (Critical issues in crime and society)
   Includes bibliographical references and index.
   ISBN 978-0-8135-4214-0 (hardcover : alk. paper)
   ISBN 978-0-8135-4215-7 (pbk. : alk. paper)
   1. Law enforcement—United States.   2. Social control—United
States.   3. Protest movements—United States.   4. Anti-globalization
movement—United States.   I. Title.
   HV8138.F454   2008
   363.32'30973—dc22   2007019967

A British Cataloging-in-Publication record for this book is available
from the British Library.

Visit our Web site: http://rutgerspress.rutgers.edu

Manufactured in the United States of America

I dedicate my book to Mare, my life partner, and to all who speak truth to power through their daily actions.

Contents

Acknowledgments   *ix*

1   *Protest, Control, and Policing*   1

2   *Perspectives on the Control of Dissent*   19

3   *The Anti-Globalization Movement*   35

4   *Managing and Regulating Protest:*
     Social Control and the Law   68

5   *This Is What Democracy Looks Like?:*
     The Physical Control of Space   92

6   *"Here Come the Anarchists":*
     The Psychological Control of Space   138

7   *Law Enforcement and Control*   165

Notes   173
Bibliography   177
Index   189

Acknowledgments

THIS BOOK COULD NEVER have been completed without the guidance, love, and encouragement of my friends and colleagues. Thank you all for participating in this collective process. I want to thank Mare Schumacher, my life partner, for her unwavering support. Her willingness to tolerate seemingly endless hours at the computer obsessing over a particular turn of phrase is deeply appreciated. Her edits, insights, and recommendations for this book were priceless. There is not enough I can do to thank her.

I am also indebted to Cecilia Menjivar. Her subtle suggestions at the start of my research made all the difference. Thank you, Randy Hanson, for lifting the curtain and showing me the wizard, reminding me that there is much beyond academia. To Beth Swadener, thank you for being an inspiration and a mentor on how to be a true scholar/activist. Also, thanks to the Society for the Study of Social Problems (and all its members) for financially supporting my research and providing an atmosphere that makes critical scholarship possible. Finally, thanks to Ray Michalowski and Adi Hovav for making editorial suggestions that greatly improved the manuscript.

A special thanks goes to Sue Hilderbrand, who ran with me in movement and stood by me when my fears got the best of me. Thanks also to Amory Starr for supporting my work. Her mentoring has been valuable. Likewise, Emily Gaarder and Randall Amster were wonderful sounding boards, providing insightful personal and intellectual feedback. In addition, my parents, Luis and Hada Luz Fernandez, played a central role getting me this far. Without their life lessons and constant emotional support, none of this would have been possible. Last (and definitely not least), I'd like to thank Rafiki and Chyna, two of the best dogs in the world. Thank you all very much. My love for all of you is unending and my appreciation deeply felt.

Policing Dissent

CHAPTER 1

Protest, Control, and Policing

You don't expect downtown Washington, D.C., to be eerily quiet and deserted. But on one Friday morning in 2002, it was. I was standing with a small group of protesters in Dupont Circle at 6:30 A.M. during the International Monetary Fund (IMF) protests. Except for our group, the police, and some morning traffic, the streets were mostly abandoned. Stores were closed; pedestrians were scarce. There was a reason. For several days, the police had warned residents to lock themselves away because "violent" protesters and anarchists would soon be taking to the streets.

The action began to pick up when members of the Pagan Cluster, with their quirky blend of nonviolence, politics, and spirituality, begin to arrive. The traffic, too, picked up; and soon the two began to intertwine. Before long, there were about seventy protestors in Dupont Circle. Surrounding the protesters were approximately one hundred officers dressed in dark Robocop-style uniforms. They wore full riot gear, including black helmets, batons, and plastic handcuffs dangling from their hips. Several held "non-lethal" weapons such as beanbags, rubber bullet rifles, and pepper spray. The combined effect of their numbers, gear, and weapons made us feel like we were in a militarized zone. In fact, the last time I remembered seeing such a scene was as a child in Nicaragua during the Sandinista Revolution. Yet the police in Nicaragua were national guards and did not seem as intimidating. Perhaps this perception was influenced by my childish view of the world, or perhaps the Nicaraguan guards were in fact less threatening than the Washington, D.C., police force. In any case, now I was face to face with a group of very intimidating law enforcement officers.

In sharp contrast to the police, the protesters wore colorful outfits without protective gear. As I've mentioned, many were members of the Pagan Cluster, a network of earth-based activists who use magic and ritual in their actions. Starhawk, a well-known pagan activist and author, stood at the center of a large circle of pagan participants orchestrating a complex ritual involving yarn, mud, and tree branches. By the end of the ritual, protesters were wearing feathers and branches on their heads, and some were covered in mud. They had also spun a large colorful yarn web that symbolized feminist struggles and the interconnected nature of human activity. Most of the members were middle-aged women with graying hair and sensible shoes. It seemed comic that a tough-looking, fully armed police force was engaged in active surveillance of a relatively small group of middle-aged women wearing feathers and mud. But the police were not amused.

When they were ready to act, the Pagan Cluster began moving the yarn web, now some twenty-five feet wide, into the street. They were careful to cross the street legally. Not knowing what to make of them, the police watched, seemingly puzzled. When the group arrived at the middle of the intersection, they promptly tied the giant web to several streetlights, effectively blocking the intersection with yarn. Cars began to honk. Drivers poked their heads out of their windows and yelled. Sirens began screeching all around us, but the protesters were undeterred. After tying the web, they took over the intersection, dancing and drumming in their colorful outfits. Starhawk led the march, calmly drumming as several protesters approached cars and said, "Sorry for the inconvenience. We are protesting globalization and the policies of the IMF. We will be gone momentarily."

Eventually, the group's actions stretched over five blocks. Police followed, warning that if members did not get off the streets, they would all be arrested. Obediently, the pagan protesters stepped onto the sidewalk. Yet soon after, the police surrounded the group and arrested everyone. It was unclear why they were arrested at that particular moment, given their obedience to police orders. Later, however, I learned that a different protest group had broken the windows of a Citibank office in another part of town, triggering preemptive arrests of all protesters, regardless of whether or not they had been engaged in peaceful protest or property destruction.

While the pagan protestors were being arrested near Dupont Circle, other protesters were practicing their right to free speech at Freedom Plaza, a few blocks away from the White House. Approximately five hundred protesters had assembled there for a drum protest, aiming to make enough noise so that people in the White House could hear their complaints against corporate globalization. Ironically (as the protesters themselves noted), the police surrounded and preemptively arrested everyone at Freedom Plaza before they could make a sound. They were charged with gathering without a permit. Reporters, legal observers, residents, and anyone else walking through the park were caught in the raid. Those arrested were held for three days and then released with the charges dropped. In short, the police took approximately six hundred protesters off the streets of Washington, D.C., for three days, effectively prohibiting them from participating in the three remaining days of planned protests.

In the Aftermath of September 11

What happened at the 2002 IMF protests probably would not have transpired in the same way before September 11, 2001.

Fear of violence, overzealous police action, and the unwilling-
ness to allow peaceful protest have become more pronounced
since 9/11. When I first started my research, the activist world
in the United States was different from what it is today. In early
2001, the anti-globalization movement was still energized from
the large 1999 World Trade Organization (WTO) protest in
Seattle and several large, well-organized mass demonstrations in
Washington, Prague, Genoa, and Quebec. As a result, radical
thought had become momentarily chic in some circles, with
anarchist and other radical collectives sprouting throughout the
United States. Mass protest became confrontational, as it had in
the sixties and seventies, with young activists refusing to comply
with protest permits and openly challenging authorities in the
streets.

This all changed after the September 11, 2001, attacks on
the World Trade Center and the Pentagon and the subsequent
adoption of the USA PATRIOT Act, when the U.S. government scaled back the civil liberties of its citizens, presumably to
increase national security. We now live with a government that
endorses the use of torture, infiltrates peace activist meetings in
churches, and routinely tracks international phone conversations. Recently, nonviolent environmental activists have been
classified as being among the nation's biggest internal terrorist
threats, and groups such as Indymedia (which stands for "independent media") are known to authorities as "radical journalists
online" (Riccardi 2006). The FBI is reportedly keeping close
watch on vegan groups and the organization known as the
Catholic Workers as well as relatively mainstream organizations
such as People for the Ethical Treatment of Animals (PETA) and
Food Not Bombs (FNB) (Lichtblau 2005). While FNB members are certainly strident in their dedication to the cause, their
most threatening activities include making and serving hummus
and pita bread to homeless people in public parks (although,
admittedly, sometimes without a permit). Keith McHenry, one

of FNB's founders, described his group to me as "people who are dedicated to change society through peaceful means." PETA's mission statement lists the following activities: "public education, cruelty investigations, research, animal rescue, legislation, special events, celebrity involvement, and protest campaigns." This description hardly sounds like terrorism: the group employs the same tactics used by religious, anti-abortion, civil rights, and countless other groups who have not been (and doubtless never will be) a threat to the safety of the United States. In fact, groups such as PETA, Indymedia, and FNB form the fabric of American democracy, exerting important external pressure on dominant political forces and sometimes forcing a national dialogue on issues that are not salient in mainstream society. Similarly, in the 1960s, the Student Nonviolent Coordinating Committee (SNCC) forced our society to confront segregation and racial inequality by using confrontational but peaceful tactics. Yet forty years later, the United States seems to be moving toward suppression of dissent and other political practices, even though these practices define our democracy.

What we are witnessing is only the tip of the iceberg. Less visible to the public are strong currents of control that operate in more subtle forms. For protests, these controls include permit negotiation, channeling mass demonstrations into protest zones, and applying legalities to subdue protest. In the case of the IMF protests, law enforcement promoted fear by warning citizens about dangerous protesters, deploying police in riot gear, and other tactics. They also used harder, more obvious forms of control, such as mass sweeps and arrests of protesters.

In this book, I examine how the state, through various law enforcement agencies, controls dissent. I examine not only direct, street-level repression but also emerging strategies beyond the street for regulation and pacification of free speech and radical thought. To understand the policing of protest, we must go beyond current ideas of repression and embrace a more dynamic

view of control and policing, including three separate but inter-
acting fields of control: the legal, physical, and psychological
fields that form around each protest. I consider each of these
fields in detail in later chapters.

THE ANTI-GLOBALIZATION
MOVEMENT AND THE POLICING
OF NETWORKS

This book is rooted in the tumultuous political activities
that make up the anti-globalization movement (also known as
the alterglobalization or anti-corporate globalization movement) and the development of new police tactics to blunt and
possibly destroy it.[1] In the past, organizations (such as labor
unions) required a centralized, hierarchical structure to operate
efficiently. The person at the top made an announcement,
which was spread through the labor lieutenants and eventually
to the workers at the bottom of the ladder. The anti-globalization
movement rejected this hierarchal scheme. Instead of a centralized system, participants adopted a decentralized, network-
based approach to political organizing and protest. Technological
advances helped to open these new organizational possibilities.
Cell phones, e-mails, and listservs allowed for more grassroots,
nonhierarchical modes of mobilization (Juris 2005). They also
allowed activists to organize through networks. Under this
scheme, multiple individuals are connected through links, creating
a vast network of ties. The anti-globalization movement, then,
represents a global network of activists with no real center and
little formal leadership. There is no Cesar Chavez, no Martin
Luther King, Jr. This mode of organizing was very effective during
the 1999 WTO protest and at several subsequent ones.

Faced with network-based movement strategies, the police
adapted their policing and social control mechanisms to manage
this new threat, targeting the very aspect of the movement that
made it successful: its network structure. Following the work of

social movement scholars such as Aldon Morris and Carol Mueller (1992), Sidney Tarrow (1998), and Marco Giugni and colleagues (1999), I assume that the state and its agents act deliberately and with thought, developing tactics and techniques for controlling those who challenge authority.[2] Like protesters, the state adjusts, adapts, and exploits opportunities as it sees fit. My task in this book is to chronicle the ways in which the state adapts to these challenges and develops new, specific forms of control that target the unique characteristics of the antiglobalization movement.

WHAT WE KNOW FROM SCHOLARS

In the past ten years, scholars have been increasingly interested in the policing of protests and its effects on social movements (McCarthy and McPhail 1997, della Porta and Reiter 1998, Waddington 1999, Schweingruber 2000). They have paid careful attention to the relationship between repression and social movement mobilization (Davenport et al. 2004), and a number of studies focus on how repression will stop or slow a social movement. For example, some scholars find that activists shift from violent to nonviolent activity when confronted with violent repression (Lichbach 1987) and that the type of state regime predicts the form of repression and how movements will respond to it (Rasler 1996). Others find different types of repression even within democratic institutions (della Porta and Reiter 1998). Some scholars argue that the role of the media is a central factor of mobilization regardless of the form of repression (Wisler and Giugni 1999), while others conclude that repression is likely to vary across police jurisdictions (McPhail and McCarthy 2004).

A similar pattern holds with scholars who work on policing. In general, they are primarily interested in understanding the triggers of protester or police violence. For instance, David Waddington and colleagues (1989) developed the flashpoint perspective to explain why some potentially disorderly events ignite while others do not. According to these authors, only a fraction of public gatherings ultimately lead to disorder or violence. The key, they argue, is to figure out what actions precipitate violence and riots. These actions are the flashpoints: dramatic breaks that tip the balance from order to disorder. Ultimately, the context of flashpoints is structural. While both social movement researchers and policing-of-protest scholars have criticized such structural perspectives (such as P.A.J. Waddington 1994), other scholars have found useful applications. Mike King and David Waddington (2005), for instance, applied the flashpoint model to two anti-globalization protests in Canada to explain why a demonstration had turned violent.

Repression is another important concept in the study of the policing of protest and is a central concern for many other scholars who study social movements (della Porta 1999, Wisler and Giugni 1999, Barkan 2001, Earl 2003, Earl et al. 2003, Davenport et al. 2004). Generally, repression refers to "any action by another group which raises the contender's cost of collective action" (Tilly 1978, 100); and as a concept, the term frames much theoretical and empirical work. For Charles Tilly, repression includes acts of harassment, intimidation, physical assault, arrests, imprisonment, and even murder.

Many studies of repression explain the conditions under which police are likely to use repressive tactics. For instance, Jennifer Earl and colleagues (2003) outline and test three distinct approaches: threat, weakness, and police agency. The threat approach posits that police are more likely to use repressive tactics when the threat to political elites increases. Thus, revolutionary and radical groups are more likely than reformist groups to experience repression (McAdam 1999). According to the weakness approach, the weaker a movement is, the more likely the state is to repress it (Gamson 1990, 1997). The police agency approach views repression as a result of internal police characteristics, as in departments with high levels of police brutality. Like much of the literature on repression, the work of Earl et al. (2003) explains *when* repression occurs, not *how* it happens. This research illuminates some patterns of repression, but it does not explore how repression operates and ignores other, more subtle forms of control.

To complement this research on causal relationships between repression and mobilization or between riots and structural factors, I shift toward an analysis of how social control works at the experiential level. I move away from the concept of repression and instead adopt the term *social control of dissent*.[3] In my view, the concept of repression, limited to overt tactics such as harassment, intimidation, assault, detainment, and murder, is too narrowly constructed and leaves out multiple spheres of contention and domination. In contrast, social control of dissent opens up the theoretical possibilities for broader studies of protest control.

Textures of Control

In the past, the state has used various forms of control to attack radical social movements that challenge its power. While control can manifest itself as harassment, arrests, and intimidations, other forms of control work in tandem with such overt tactics. In my research, I have observed two different modes of control. The first is hard-line social control, which includes the tactics used by the FBI or dictatorships to directly undermine and abolish movements. Hard-line social control is the primary focus of many scholars who study and document the effects of repression. For instance, the events during the 2002 IMF protest in Washington, D.C., exemplified hard-line repression in the sense that police arrested and physically removed people from the streets.

The second mode, soft-line social control, includes more indirect forms of oppression, such as the control of dissent through legal regulation, negotiation of protest, and self-monitoring. Soft-line social control is more subtle and thus harder to study.

Scholars are now exploring the ways in which this softer method works. For instance, Myra Marx Ferree (2004) looks at what she calls *soft repression* as it affects gender-based movements, arguing that "the concept of repression is bound up with a state-centered view of social movements. . . . Repression is what states do, specifically bad states that cannot manage dissent in more democratic and disarming ways" (138). She uses the term to describe the mobilization of nonviolent means to silence, discredit, or eliminate oppositional ideas. Soft repression assumes a negative notion of power—one that inhibits and restrains, albeit in a pliable manner. I prefer the term *soft-line social control* because it includes nonrepressive social control mechanisms; in other words, it refers as well to the positive, productive aspects of state power.

CONTROL AND SOCIAL MOVEMENTS

Scholars who examine social protests have two other areas of study. The first is the study of the effects of the law on social movements or repression as the primary consequence of legal control (Barkan 2001). While this literature provides insight into state practices, it focuses primarily on the hard-line side of legal repression, almost ignoring the soft-line tactics of legal control, such as the use of legal permits.

Otto Kirchheimer's (1980) *Political Justice* is a classic study of legal repression. He documents several cases in which state powers used the courts to lend a cloak of legality to their repressive tactics. In such cases, the legal system becomes a political tool used, in the most extreme cases, to incriminate, discredit, and imprison political foes. Successfully applied to a social movement, such tactics remove leaders and scare newcomers from participating in future movement work and send a chilling warning to those involved in the movement.[4]

Kirchheimer shows that court trials can also further the cause of a social movement, but these legal battles may have unintended detrimental consequences. Using the courts to challenge the system can have a negative impact on the movement, forcing activists to spend much time, money, and energy on their legal defense—resources that could be spent in other ways (Rosenberg 1991, Barkan 2001). Importantly, Kirchheimer's work points out that the legal system is not a neutral apparatus but a process that can be used for political gain. He looks, however, mainly at legal cases after a protest, saying little about how the law is applied before or during a protest.

Isaac Balbus's (1973) *The Dialectics of Legal Repression* is often cited for its analysis of the legal control of social movements. Examining the U.S. urban riots of the 1960s, Balbus finds that legal repression typically takes the form of massive arrests followed by the complete dismissal of charges (a tactic still used today). He sees the legal system as not just courts and political parties but also arrests and other police functions. By noting that it reduces threats to the state, he shows us the ideological functions and consequences of legal control.

Building on the work of Kirchheimer and Balbus, Steven Barkan (2001) argues that legal repression is at times an effective tool for stifling protest and dissent. He provides several examples, including the repression of dissent during World War I, when laws prohibited any criticism of the war. In the case of the civil rights movement, Barkan (1984) finds that while the federal legal system (for example, the Supreme Court) ruled in favor of the movement grievances, state and local laws were exceedingly repressive. In short, he shows that law can be a tool of control.

Ward Churchill and Jim Vander Wall (2002) describe the more aggressive side of legal repression. Their work documents the extensive history of oppressive campaigns against political dissent, dating as far back as 1920. For example, shortly after World War I, the FBI undertook the Palmer Raids, which targeted the anarchist and anarcho-syndicalist movements.

Fifteen thousand people were arrested overnight, primarily because they were recent immigrants to the United States. Each person was questioned regarding subscriptions to radical magazines and involvement in radical organizations; the result was mass deportation to the Soviet Union without a hearing. There is an eerie resemblance between the Palmer Raids and the more recent FBI roundup of Arab men after the terrorist attacks on the World Trade Center. At times, old tactics come back under a different guise with new justifications. Churchill discusses several other examples of movement suppression, such as the attack on the International Workers of the World, the United Negro Improvement Association, the Communist party, and the Black Panthers. He details the FBI's various tactics, including the discrediting of movement leaders, infiltration, agents provocateurs, the manufacturing of legal evidence, and assassination (Churchill 2002).

The second area of study focuses on the process of policing and its effects on social movements (McCarthy and McPhail 1997, della Porta and Reiter 1998, P.A.J. Waddington 1999). Donna della Porta and Herbert Reiter (1998) argue that police used an escalated force model to manage protest before and during the 1960s. This model is characterized by intolerant, sometimes illegal, hard-line modes of policing. In the 1970s, under significant pressure to modify the aggressive tactics that had led to urban uprisings in a number of American cities, police shifted toward a softer, more tolerant model known as negotiated management.

When following the escalated force model, police show little tolerance for community disruption and often enforce the law too vigorously, heavily harassing protesters (Schweingruber 2000). Police see themselves as the protectors of order, entrusted to maintain the law and protect private property from lawless protesters. They keep a distance from protesters, viewing demonstrators' actions as illegitimate and individual protesters as deviant. There is no negotiation before, during, or after a protest; and contact with protesters is reduced to arrest, arraignment, and confinement (McPhail and McCarthy 2004). The primary tactic of control is force, including beatings, the use of attack dogs, and indiscriminate mass arrest (McPhail et al. 1998). The goal is to suppress dissent by all means possible. As a result, protesters suffer violations of freedom-of-speech rights as well as more serious injury and psychological trauma. Scholars point to the riots outside the 1968 Democratic National Convention in Chicago as an example of this type of policing (McCarthy and McPhail 1997). While the approach can inhibit mobilization, it also can have significant negative consequences for the establishment by creating adverse publicity for the state and sympathy for the protesters. For example, P.A.J. Waddington (1994) shows that negative media coverage sometimes results in administrative changes in police departments or city leadership. If the public views such overt violence as illegitimate, high-level administrators and city leaders may suffer unpleasant consequences.

Since the 1980s, police departments in North America and Europe have frequently turned to the negotiated management model, which shifts away from the indiscriminate use of force. According to John David McCarthy and Clark McPhail (1997), the key to this approach is to respect protesters' claim to the First Amendment. When they properly apply the model, police offer movement leaders concessions in exchange for an agreement to self-police and to outline the scale, route, and timing of demonstrations (McCarthy and McPhail 1997, McPhail et al. 1998). The negotiation process between police and protesters begins when social movement organizers request a legal permit to march or gather in public areas. Once this request is made, police rely on constant communication to gather as much information as possible about the protest, which helps them maintain order once the protest is in the street. Several scholars have documented this type of policing behavior (P.A.J. Waddington

1994, McCarthy and McPhail 1997, della Porta and Reiter 1998, Davenport et al. 2004).

McPhail and colleagues (1998) argue that the permit process is key to the negotiated management model because it creates a bureaucratic process that requires protesters to engage in dialogue. The permit process requires a long list of information, including the name of the person and organization applying for the permit; the time, date, and location of the protest; a list of speakers and activities; the number of people expected; what kinds of props will be used; the number and training of demonstration marshals who are expected to control the protesters; and the likelihood and identity of any counter-demonstrators. In sum, the permit process forces protesters to negotiate their presence on the street.

ANOTHER PERSPECTIVE ON CONTROL

To properly understand the social control of dissent, we must take a critical view of both the negotiated management model and the notion of repression. Rather than seeing the negotiated model as a way of "protecting protestors' First Amendment and human rights" (McPhail and McCarthy 2004, 5), I see it as equally about regulating, managing, and pacifying dissent. It is not merely concerned about providing "sufficient openness in the reciprocal statements of ends and means [so] that both parties [police and protesters] can negotiate a mutually agreed-upon game plan" (6). As I will demonstrate in the following chapters, the negotiated model favors the police and acts as a form of soft-line social control. The information gathered through the permit process not only allows police to plan for and control demonstrations but also makes tactics (such as sit-ins, blockades, and traffic disruption) less likely to occur and more costly to the protesters in terms of arrests and prosecution and makes mobilizing people more difficult. More important, it is a form of passive coercion in which the rules, as outlined by the police, become part of the working practices of the movement organizers. When applied tactically, the organizers become complicit in producing less contentious protest actions.

The effectiveness of the negotiated model is evident in the institutionalization of protest in the United States during the 1980s. In that period, organizers from various movements (for instance, the anti-nuclear and peace movements) readily adopted the negotiated management model. They regularly and willingly negotiated the locations of protest, making arrangements for symbolic arrests. It became common for marches and rallies to include "peacekeepers"—members of the protesting group who watched over the crowd to ensure safety and compliance with previously agreed-upon conduct. This internalized self-control resulted in protests that were easily tolerated by the state.

Yet in the mid- to late 1990s, groups associated with what would become the current anti-globalization movement began to reject police negotiations and adopted more confrontational tactics. Some groups used nonhierarchical styles of organizing, confronted the police, and challenged the more institutionalized and passive nature of the 1980s movements. As a result of the shift in protest tactics, the police developed more sophisticated modes of control that are neither purely repressive nor entirely negotiated. Rather, the current mode is an effective mixture of hard- and soft-line tactics, including the use of new "non-lethal weapons" as well as laws, codes, regulations, and public relations strategies that attempt to control protest spaces directly and indirectly.

In sum, policing and social movement scholars tend to look at control mainly in terms of either repression (such as arrests, incarceration, murder) or the negotiated management model. My research adds a new perspective to the study of social movements and control. Rather than seeing control as either purely repressive or purely managerial, I argue that hard- and soft-line modes of social control coexist. To understand how the social control of dissent operates, I expand the current concepts and focus on individual protests to get a closer view of the wide range of control practices.

DATA AND BOOK STRUCTURE

My research originates from several years of participatory observation in the anti-globalization movement, in which I employed a *verstehen* approach to capture the effects of social control on the mind, body, and social relationships of protesters.[5] From 2001 to 2005, I took part in several large protests in North America. I gathered data through multiple ethnographic methods, including participatory observation, semi-structured interviews with law enforcement and anti-globalization activists, and reviews of newspaper articles and police documents associated with various protests.

I present my findings in the following six chapters. In Chapter 2, I examine several theories of social control and its relation to mass protest, starting with classic understandings of coercion and ending with an analysis of Michel Foucault's concept of biopower and governmentality. Building on his theories as well as Michael Hardt and Antonio Negri's notion of the multitude, I argue that the new forms of social control that have emerged in recent years are directly implicated in the policing of this network-based movement. In Chapter 3, I chronicle the anti-globalization movement and its context, describing both its historical specificity and its unique, nonhierarchical internal structure. I begin with a general discussion of the grievances expressed against globalization and then examine the movement itself, describing its unique structure. Finally, I show that the flat configuration of the movement requires a specific method of control.

Chapters 4, 5, and 6 provide detailed accounts of the social control of dissent. Each chapter explores one of three aspects of control, which are distinct but overlapping. Chapter 4 considers how the state employs legal techniques to restrict the movement of protesters. I show how law enforcement agencies use ordinances, city codes, and state laws to inhibit mobilization, demonstrating that legal control of protest is wider and more diffuse than the current literature suggests. Chapter 5 describes how police manipulate the physical space around a protest to control movement. I describe the lengthy planning process that law enforcement professionals undertake months before an anti-globalization protest, showing that control starts when law enforcement carefully selects and maps the geographical space of a protest. I contend that this planning process and physical manipulation of space is designed specifically to contend with the network-based aspects of the anti-globalization movement. Chapter 6 explores the cultural practices and politics of policing dissent, shifting the focus to psychological aspects of control. The psychological sphere includes the use of public media campaigns that frame the movement. Building on the concept of securitization, the chapter depicts how law enforcement capitalizes on terrorism to induce a heightened sense of fear in both activist and the general populations. When framed properly, this heightened sense of fear allows police to use an escalated model of policing, if they deem necessary, with little public resistance. I then analyze the concrete cultural practices and micro-politics through which the state controls the meaning of a protest.

Finally, in Chapter 7, I analyze the impact of new control strategies on the anti-globalization movement and what they mean for the future policing of protest. The chapter begins with a brief overview of the legal, physical, and psychological aspects of control, showing how they can operate in conjunction to form a larger field of control. I then trace the origins of this larger field to changes in the mode of control resulting from the flat, network-based, and nonhierarchical organizational style of the anti-globalization movement. The chapter presents an analysis of security and the state's role in policing these international protests, concluding that, at least in the realm of national security,

the state is solidifying its power and not "lessening in importance" as some globalization scholars have predicted. In closing,
I critique previous scholarship of protest policing, primarily
studies of the negotiated management model.

My Approach

I do not aim to provide a definitive statement on how all social
movements are policed or even on how the anti-globalization
movement is policed everywhere. Rather, I examine how control
operated during five protests. By design, I theorized not from the
perspective of the state or from a purely academic point of view
but from the perspective of those who are most affected by control
and repression. To that end, I entered the movement and
immersed myself in it, looking to feel, see, and hear what social
control does to the mind and body.

While my work is ethnographic, it does not directly reflect
how activists feel during a protest. Yet many of the ideas presented here originate from personal experiences in the field. For
instance, my insights on the production of fear came not from
the literature but from moments of terror while police surrounded and fired upon many of my friends. My analysis deals
with how control operates, presenting empirical accounts of
what activists currently experience as they seek to make social
change.

Nevertheless, a word of caution is in order. As I documented the state's exercise of control, I intentionally left out
much of the resistance exercised by anti-globalization activists.
As a result, I risk making the state look all-powerful, full of
agency, and unchallenged. The truth could not be more different. For every tactic described here, activists ingeniously developed ways to resist. Nevertheless, the state's new forms of
control are less obvious than protesters' actions. For this reason,
I focused my work primarily on the side of state control, hoping
to offer meaningful insights in this area.

CHAPTER 2

Perspectives on the Control of Dissent

As a concept, social control has a life of its own. Much has been written about it from sociological, criminological, political, and postmodern perspectives. Scholars use the term in studies of such diverse topics as deviance (Cohen 1966, Little 1989), punishment (Blomberg and Cohen 2003), disputes and the rule of law (Lauderdale and Cruit 1993), and science and technology in postindustrial society (Hier 2003, Lianos 2003). My purpose in this chapter is not to definitively review all these scholarly considerations of social control. Rather, I present a theoretical framework bridging political, sociological, and postmodern views of social control to investigate the state's tactics for controlling dissent and radical movements.

AN OVERVIEW OF SOCIAL CONTROL

According to Thomas Blomberg and Stanley Cohen (2003), theories of social control originate in classical political and social theory. Thomas Hobbes, Jean-Jacques Rousseau, and John Locke, for instance, focus on the emergence of the liberal democratic state. Each grapples with how governments rule (or control) their citizens while protecting their natural rights and liberties. They link social control to the rise of the state and citizenship as well as the state's ability to administer appropriate force to ensure social order. This is particularly the case in the work of Hobbes (1991), who argues that the sovereign (such as a ruler or a government) is principally responsible for maintaining order through force in order to secure the social contract. For Hobbes, social control means the state's ability to maintain a stable citizenship so that society does not regress to a brutal condition of nature.

More contemporary theorists see the police as an entity designed to mitigate social order and maintain a stable citizenry. Stemming from this line of thought is the argument that police help the sovereign (or the state) beget good social order. That is, the police as a body administers regulations to maintain the internal social order of the community (Neocleous 2000). The concept of the police emerged with the decline of feudalism in sixteenth-century Europe, coinciding with the growth of the modern state and an increasing concern for maintaining social order. "As the established and customary relations of the feudal world began to collapse, the old systems of authority were increasingly undermined. New means and practices for the constitution of political order were necessary and thus new concepts with which to understand them. In its origins, 'police' thus presupposes a breakdown of the state-based order which had previously given form to the social body" (2). Because the concepts of both social control and the police appeared during the transition from feudalism to modernity and emanated from a concern for state security, discussion of social control has, from the beginning, been connected to the security of the state. Thus, a study dealing with political dissent must center on the state and take the police as a primary point of study.

Social control has a slightly different meaning in the sociological literature, which concentrates on social conformity. In the early twentieth century, American sociologists began to examine the integration of society and the process of conformity. They viewed social control as a form of internal compliance to societal norms. Rather than looking at social control as a function of the state, they examined other social institutions as purveyors of order, including the family, churches, neighborhoods, and personal beliefs.

Much early academic work on social control attempts to understand both deviance and social order. As it is generally understood, deviance is behavior that differs from socially acceptable norms. Deviant acts include criminal behavior, such as stealing and murder, as well as what some consider to be less severe behaviors, such as using drugs and viewing pornography. One early and influential school of thought developed at the Chicago School of Sociology, where researchers such as Robert Park, Ernest W. Burgess, and Herbert Blumer conceived of social control as a process rather than a structure (Goode 2001). For them, it was not laws or state authority that mattered but the level of organization of a given city, neighborhood, peer group, or gang (Blomberg and Cohen 2003). Disorganization, or the breakdown of social order, results when community norms are no longer strong enough to enforce social control.

The functionalist approach is another angle to dealing with social order. This classic theory conceptualizes society as an organism with multiple parts, each functioning separately to balance the larger system. Proponent Talcott Parsons argued that social order is carried on through a series of interactional systems, which include personality and cultural systems. For functionalists, social order is maintained through tolerance of social disorder—specifically, when the disorder in question serves a functional role in society.

Labeling theory offers a more contemporary sociological approach to social control and deviance (Becker 1963, Pfohl 1994). Closely associated to symbolic interactionism, this approach argues that human behavior is relative, interpretive, and best understood in human interactions. In other words, meaning is a negotiated process: it is created rather than absolute and independent. In turn, deviant behavior is also an interpretive process. Therefore, what society holds as deviant behavior depends on the meaning and interpretation given to an act rather than the act itself. Important to this school of thought is who is labeled deviant and how deviant behavior changes in a fluid and pluralistic society. Labeling theory is useful because it moves toward the productive ideas of power, a critical concept for interpreting control and dissent. The theory looks at how behavior is labeled as deviant, understanding that the process of labeling is also a process of construction. The idea is helpful for looking at the policing of protests because it suggests that what are considered acceptable and unacceptable forms of protest change over time, depending on context and historical period. Thus, protest is a fluid category—sometimes allowed, sometimes repressed.

Conflict is the final social control theory I discuss here. Derived from Marxist analysis, conflict theory sees social control primarily as class domination. That is, it rejects the idea that laws are designed to protect the rights of all members of a given society. Instead, proponents argue that laws and the interests of the dominant or hegemonic classes drive social control at both moral and legal levels (Quinney 2001). The role of the police and the law becomes imposition, forcing a social order that benefits those at the top of the social hierarchy. As with labeling theory, power plays a significant role in explaining social control.

A common thread runs through much of the sociological literature of social control: a consideration of formal and informal practices (Goode 2001). Informal social control processes maintain general societal order through non-state organizations, such as the family and churches. If these forms of control do not work, however, then more formal means are employed. That is, when the family or neighborhood can no longer induce a sense of obligation on individuals, then the state uses more coercive means, which may include the police and other state agencies as well as laws and punitive punishment. Whether looked at through a political or a sociological lens, social control is always linked to the maintenance of social order.[1] Both perspectives share the idea that, without social order, we risk disorder and possibly the end of society. Thus, the mechanisms of social control, whether formal or informal, cultural or legal, are justified as security.

SOCIAL CONTROL OF DISSENT

My research focuses on one application of social control: the regulation and pacification of protesters. I examine how the state employs force, intimidation, and negotiation to subvert the power of people in the street and limit protest's potential impact on the status quo. Thus, my theoretical framework blurs the boundaries between political and sociological approaches. In tune with political scientists, I see protest as a phenomenon that inherently involves the state and the idea of security. I am not arguing that protesters only and necessarily target government or its agencies. Rather, I believe that law enforcement agencies are primarily responsible for maintaining order, and these organizations are strongly linked to the state. This is particularly true in the anti-globalization movement, in which protesters target hypergovernmental agencies such as the World Trade Organization, the World Bank, and the International Monetary Fund. Those responsible for policing protest are a mixture of policing and intelligence agencies firmly associated with the nation–state apparatus but who also articulate missions, activities, and strategies beyond the nation–state.

From the general sociological perspective, we see that the state employs social control techniques that work productively to maintain the social order. This idea provides insight on how the policing of protest works. That is, like deviance, acceptable and unacceptable forms of protest change over time and produce political deviance. As I will show in Chapter 5, for instance, laws have changed specifically to control the anti-globalization movement, at times producing political deviance where it did not exist previously. It is important to note here that political deviance (like other forms of deviance) is socially constructed.

POWER, BIOPOWER, AND GOVERMENTALITY

Postmodern scholars borrow from the work of Michel Foucault in their studies of social control (Lyon 2002, Lianos 2003, Wood 2003).[2] Examining surveillance and other technologies, they have situated control in a post-Fordist or flexible labor society. To clarify their theories, I will briefly review Foucault's contributions, starting with his concept of power. Following Friedrich Nietzsche, Foucault inverted traditional notions of power to show how power operates at the microlevel (Sarup 1993). Traditionally, political scientists define power as an individual's or institution's ability to coerce another into behavior or actions in which they would not otherwise engage. According to this definition, power is coercive and forceful; yet Foucault (1973, 1988, 1995) also points out that power is about categorizing, producing sexuality, and internalizing discipline. In other words, power has a productive capacity. It is able to coerce; but more importantly, it produces docile bodies through surveillance, regulation, and discipline.

Central to Foucault's work are concepts of power, knowledge, and the body. For him, as well as Gilles Deleuze and Felix Guattari (1988), the body is the object on which power and domination apply force. That is, systems of control rely on the ability to subjugate bodies, rendering them docile, obedient, and useful (Garland 1990). It is not difficult to see that the domination of the body is also central in the policing of protest, where many techniques of control rely on the police's ability to render protesters docile. Foucault outlines four general types of technologies of control. First are the technologies of production, which aim at controlling, transforming, and manipulating objects and raw materials. Second are the technologies of sign systems, which involve the production of symbols and signification. Third are the technologies of power, which determine the conduct of individuals and submit them to certain ends or dominations. Fourth are the technologies of the self, by which individuals modify their own souls, thoughts, conduct, and ways of being (Foucault et al. 1988). According to Foucault, these four technologies hardly ever function separately.

While Karl Marx (1970, 1977) focused on interpreting the interaction between technologies of production and the self, showing how changes in production modify individual conduct, Foucault was interested in interactions between the technologies of power (or domination) and the self. To understand this interaction (which Foucault terms *governmentality*) we must first examine *biopower*. The word refers generally to the exercise of control over the human body at the anatomical and biological levels. Biopower can emanate from national policies (such as abortion policies or capital punishment), but it aims at not only controlling individual behavior but also producing entire populations. Foucault connected the emergence of biopower to the state's ability to use statistical technologies to understand and study its citizenry (Foucault et al. 1988), with the goal of implementing policies that enable productive citizens to fit larger economic needs. The beauty of the approach, according to Foucault, is that the citizenry is not forced to adapt. Rather, they adapt out of self-interest, rendering the process of control partly a matter of self-regulation. Thus, biopower is a process of internalized production and reproduction. Michael Hardt and Antonio Negri (2000) explain biopower as "a form of power that regulates social life from its interior, following it, interpreting it, absorbing it, and rearticulating it" (24). In short, biopower is the power over life itself. It includes the ability to administer the life of an entire social body by increasing order, organization, and police control (Atterton 1994).

In sum, we know that techniques of domination work predominantly on the body by classifying and objectifying individuals. They operate in places such as prisons, hospitals, and schools, working not only by coercion or force but also by producing individuals who internalize modes of control out of self-interest. The concept of governmentality combines the technologies of domination and the self. Thus, according to Foucault, we learn and produce docile bodies ourselves. More precisely, we internalize what it means to be a citizen in a democracy and then police our own behavior. The same is true in respect to protest.

In Foucault's work, governmentality means the art of government, or the reason of state. Reason here "refers to the state, to its nature and to its own rationality" (Foucault et al. 1988, 150). The logic of the state is perpetuation and the reproduction of its own authority. The technologies of domination, then, become the means by which the state renders individuals as elements for the state. Rather than purely representing the interest of citizens, the government produces a citizenry that is manageable and easy to govern. Because humans have a strong tendency to revolt and resist, the state is not always able to succeed. Nevertheless, it is more or less effective.

By *government* Foucault (1983) does not mean a representative ruling body but an entity that exists for its own sake and is involved with "the conduct of conduct" (208). Government does more than legislate and rule; it also shapes, guides, and affects the conduct of people. The citizenry internalizes proper conduct and behaves accordingly. This last point is particularly relevant to the study of the social control of dissent: when examining the policing of protest according to Foucault's insights, we should expect to find both coercive power and productive aspects of the state apparatus. As I show in subsequent chapters, the state does indeed use approaches that shape the meaning of what it means to be a protester. For instance, through regulatory mechanisms such as protest permits and negotiations, it is able to create "good" and "bad" protesters. Protesters internalize these constructions to police and regulate their own behavior as well as the behavior of their fellow protesters.

Based on Foucault's insights into the study of control and domination, I view power not only as property to be won by a particular class but also as a strategy implemented at specific points in time. Power is, above all, a position, tactic, maneuver, and strategy (Deleuze and Hand 1988). It is about the meticulous regimentation of time, space, and the human body. Power is diffused and decentralized and spreads throughout institutions. Rather than being homogeneous, it is specifically employed, appearing and disappearing in relation to the object it attempts to control. Above all, power is most visible and productive in social spaces and on human bodies—for instance, in the policing of protest.

Policing the Multitude

As Hardt and Negri (2000) and others (such as Vahamaki 2004) note, labor has transformed over the past thirty years from material to immaterial. Society has moved from a factory-based system to become a knowledge society, where the production of knowledge is the ultimate commodity. Although this concept may seem to be unrelated to policing dissent, the shift in production is directly linked to the changing modes of control.

According to Marx (1977), society's central organizational principle is labor. Foucault adds that the organization of labor works in specific spaces (such as factory, office, or hospital) and through biopower as it produces a subject able and willing to operate in these spaces. Extending Foucault's argument, Jussi Vahamaki (2004) argues that we are moving toward a new organizational principle: away from factory work toward more flexible labor practices. Labor is becoming a psychological entity, and the state is now adapting so that it can "govern and control the labor force as mental entity" (223).

To elucidate the effects of this shift, let us consider the meanings of mental, or immaterial, labor. In *Empire*, Hardt and Negri (2000) use the concept to explain political and social changes in large social movements. In their eyes, it results from a service-based economy: "Since the production of services results in no material and durable good, we define the labor involved in this production as immaterial labor—that is, labor that produces immaterial goods, such as services, a cultural product, knowledge, or communication" (290).

This "informational economy" shifts from the production of physical goods to the production of nonmaterial products.[3] Hardt and Negri spell out three different types of immaterial labor:

> The first is involved in an industrial production that has been informationalised and has incorporated communication technologies in a way that transforms the production process itself. Manufacturing is regarded as a service, and the material labour of the production of durable goods mixes with and tends toward immaterial labor. Second is the immaterial labor of analytical and symbolic tasks, which itself breaks down into creative and intelligent manipulation on the one hand and routine symbolic tasks on the other. Finally, a third type of immaterial labor involves the production and manipulation of affect and requires (virtual or actual) human contact, labor in the bodily mode. These are three types of labor that drive the postmodernisation of the global economy. (293)

In sum, immaterial work produces immaterial products, such as ideas, information, images, relationships, and affects. The postindustrial economy, the authors argue, has commodified knowledge, information, and communication.

In *Multitude*, a follow-up to *Empire*, Hardt and Negri (2004) expand on the concept of immaterial labor, breaking it down into characteristics. First, immaterial labor moves from the economic realm and spreads to the creation of both social and biological life. For instance, it is closely connected to flexible working environments, where work is service-oriented, part-time, and performed in virtual space. This shift, along with changes in management styles, has blurred the lines between home and office, work and recreation, and self and organization. When considering the creation of biological life, Vandana Shiva and other scholars have chronicled how corporations are manipulating living organisms, placing patents on them, and claiming them as corporate property (Fowler 1995, Shiva and Moser 1995, Shiva 1997). Shiva (1997) also shows that immaterial labor is related to developing legal strategies (such as intellectual property rights) that rank claim of discovery or ownership of an idea over indigenous knowledge accumulated through thousands of years of experience. What we previously thought of as nature (seeds, cells, and the reproductive cycle) is now human labor and invention, making it eligible for ownership. Immaterial labor, then, produces new subjectivities and mechanisms for the exploitation of social spheres that were previously free from commodification. According to Shiva (1997), this new commodification is a neocolonial practice: the exploitation of indigenous and poor people by those who understand and can manipulate intellectual property rights and other by-products of immaterial labor.

A second characteristic of immaterial labor is that it takes "the form of networks based on communication, collaboration, and affective communication" (Hardt and Negri 2004, 66). Immaterial labor constantly invents new forms of collaboration for its production; and according to Hardt and Negri, its ability to produce networks leads to exciting possibilities. Taking a Marxist perspective, they seek a population that can challenge postmodern capitalism, and they find it in the shifting nature of labor itself. They call this population the *multitude*. Hardt and

Negri use the concept to replace what is generally understood as the people or the proletariat, which, they argue, have played a central role in past resistance movements. Both concepts rely on a centralized idea of power that melds individuals into a larger organizational body and historically have mainly been used as phrases to validate the ruling authority. In contrast, Hardt and Negri use the notion of multitude to suggest the grouping of singularities who discover what they have in common with each other without fusing into a sovereign unit.

The multitude, according to these authors, is a natural consequence of immaterial labor. Like industrialization's production of the proletariat, new economic arrangements (which are no longer purely economic) have produced the multitude. The information economy produces individuals who can work independently and are oriented toward consumerism. They are the seeds of a new struggling class, and a first step in the formation of this class is recognition of what they have in common.

Is the multitude possible? Does it have revolutionary potential? Hardt and Negri answer yes on both counts. As they see it, the anti-globalization movement is one example. For these authors, the multitude reflects a multiplicity of subjects. It is neither a unit nor a coherent group. Rather, it is like an infinite number of points, differentiated but able to work together (Vahamaki 2004). "The multitude . . . is legion; it is composed of innumerable elements that remain different, one from the other, and yet communicate, collaborate, and act in common" (Hardt and Negri 2004, 140). What brings it together is the realization of *the common*, which Hardt and Negri describe as that which we all share, along with the ability to communicate and act together.[4] The common does not arise from a unifying reality, which you would expect from crude Marxist materialism. Rather, it is created out of the information society, which requires subjectivities that emphasize singularity and collaboration. Our new economic arrangements bring about the possibility of the common.

The idea of the common is directly linked to Deleuze and Guattari's (1988) rhizomatic logic of singularities and connections and to concrete organizing practice and action in the anti-globalization movement. Hardt and Negri (2004) argue that immaterial labor and its tendency to produce social life through a growing network creates the common. Ultimately, this means that all social life is being produced collectively, as a rhizome.[5]

Following this logic, then, we see that the multitude takes on a second definition. The multitude is a concept of class, a grouping produced by the immaterial nature of labor. This class, however, does not unify people or require class-consciousness. The multitude is not a base or a section of society. We no longer have a purely economic sphere or base because economic production can no longer be distinguished from culture or leisure. If capitalism is sustained through the expropriation of human labor, then capitalism expropriates everything in a postindustrial or information economy—not only economic goods but also all parts of the biopolitical, including ideas, emotions, and life itself.

So what do immaterial labor, the multitude, and the common have to do with social control and the policing of dissent? Everything! The changing nature of labor and the emergence of the multitude open spaces and possibilities for new forms of resistance. Because resistance and social control go hand in hand, they also trigger new forms of control. I see the resistance and control process as a loop: late capitalism forms subjectivities that make the multitude possible; then the potential of the multitude as resistance requires the state to adopt and create new practices for control. The state adapts to new forms of resistance, developing practical tactics to mitigate the network-based movements that challenge its power.

What I examine in this book can be thought of as the policing of the multitude. While some scholars are focusing on control and the multitude (Vahamaki 2004), none have thus far used empirical research to describe how the state controls the multitude as it appears in the context of global bureaucratic institutions (which I call *globacracies*) such as the World Trade Organization and the International Monetary Fund.[6] My goal is to show how the state is coming to terms with the threat of the multitude; how it polices singularities; and how it controls decentralized, nonhier-archical, rhizomatic movements.

LEGAL, PHYSICAL, AND PSYCHOLOGICAL SPHERES

To study the problem of control, I use a grounded theoret-ical approach based on participatory observation, a method described further in Chapter 3. Thus, what I note as legal, phys-ical, and psychological spheres of control stem from data analy-sis, not from the social control literature. Studying these spheres both individually and interactively creates a nuanced picture of the social control of dissent.

As I have discussed, the social control of dissent deals specifi-cally with how the state uses power in the face of protest. To clar-ify this process, I divide the control of protest into three spheres (primarily for heuristic reasons), keeping in mind Pierre Bourdieu's

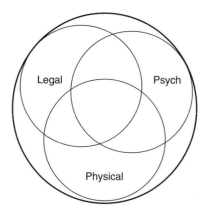

2-1. The social control of dissent.

(1984) notion of social fields: arenas of competition in which actors strategize and employ tactics to gain economic, social, and or economic capital. As I see it, a protest sphere is a location in which protesters and police contend for power. In such areas of contention, social actors interact in strategic ways, using tactics to gain protest capital, such as favorable public opinion or ability to disrupt the order. My three protest spheres are not mutually exclusive. Rather, they work in tandem and are intricately connected in maintaining a diffused, systemic form of control—a larger protest field. The legal, physical, and psychological spheres of control work at different levels and involve different techniques of control, which the state uses at different times and in different spaces.

Other scholars have also used Bourdieu's concept of social fields in the study of protest. For instance, Raka Ray (1999) adopts the concept to examine two women's movements in India. Ray defines a field of protest as a "structured, unequal, and socially constructed environment with which organizations are embedded and to which organizations constantly respond" (6). It is a configuration of forces and sites of struggle, a general space that includes all the actors, resources, and strategies available for contention. I see the field of the social control of dissent as the broader setting in which actors struggle over protest capital. Within this field are the legal, physical, and psychological spheres of control. These subfields are individually structured and work in specific social environments.

The legal sphere of control refers to how the state uses legal techniques to regulate, manage, and pacify the anti-globalization movement. It involves tactics such as city ordinances and codes, zoning restrictions, and march-permit processes. Actors may include the police, city councils, fire departments, and other staff in charge of implementing city regulations. This sphere of control starts functioning months before a protest, when movement organizers seek permits and building facilities from the city hosting the protest.

The physical sphere refers to the control of large groups of people in a given physical space. It incorporates the movement of bodies on the street and the mapping of physical and social spaces so that protesters are subdued as much as possible. This sphere necessarily involves various forms of police maneuvering before and during a mass demonstration. Actors include assemblages of police officers such as snatch squads, bicycle police, and riot personnel.[7]

The psychological sphere of control refers to the struggle over the meaning of a protest. It involves the attitudes, fears, and uncertainties of radical protesters. It is the process whereby such feelings are produced. My focus, however, is not on the feelings of protesters *per se* but on the mechanisms that produce those feelings. The psychological sphere is where meaning is fought over and where public opinion is created. Actors include various protest organizations, police, public information bureaus, media agencies, and public relations firms.

While I analyze each sphere separately, in reality they together weave the fabric of the social control of dissent. For instance, the media campaign that police unleash in the months before a protest unfolds alongside the revision of city codes aimed to regulate protesters. At the same time, law enforcement officers map out the physical space where the protests will take place. Each sphere is operating simultaneously in an attempt to reduce the impact of dissent.

CHAPTER 3

The Anti-Globalization
Movement

STUDYING THE CONTROL of the anti-globalization movement is daunting because the movement seems to be everywhere and nowhere at the same time. Taking on the characteristics of a multitude, the movement appears throughout the world in surprising locations. Social movement scholars see it in the water wars of Cochabamba, Peru (Shiva 2002), in the Zapatista struggle in Mexico (Hayden 2002), in indigenous resistance to genetically modified agriculture (Kimbrell 2002), in the peasant occupation of lands in Brazil (Wright and Wolford 2003), and even in the protest against gentrification in downtown Tempe, Arizona (Amster 2004). The anti-globalization movement is also located in labor disputes over free-trade agreements (Brecher et al. 2000), in the fight against sweatshop labor (Fung et al. 2001), and in the symbolic manipulation of corporate symbols (Klein 2000).

Characteristically, there is little agreement on the origins of the movement. Some feel it sprang from the 1999 World Trade Organization protest in Seattle (Yuen et al. 2001). Others see its roots in the struggles of American gay activists in the 1980s; in "reclaiming the streets" protests in New York and London during the same decade (Shepard and Hayduk 2002); or in the International Monetary Fund riots in Asia, Latin America, and Africa some thirty years ago (Woodroffe 2000). Still others believe that the movement was born five hundred years ago, when the indigenous people of the Americas fought European colonizers (Notes from Nowhere 2003).

Clearly, there is a wide variety of opinion on what constitutes the movement and its origins. It is also clear, however, that studying all of these spaces simultaneously is impossible. Restricted by travel expenses, time constraints, language barriers, and basic common sense, I focus in this book only on North America, including Mexico, the United States, and Canada. I consciously (and cautiously) locate the movement as it confronts, through protest, those global and regional institutions whose main task is to promote, develop, or implement corporate globalization through neoliberal free-market policies. These globacracies include the International Monetary Fund (IMF), the World Bank (WB), the World Trade Organization (WTO), the Free Trade of the Americas Agreement (FTAA), as well as lesser known groups such as the Group of Eight (G8) and the World Economic Forum (WEF), where global elites meet to discuss global market policies.

I also focus primarily on the street side of the protests. Excluded from this study are the internal and reformist efforts of anti-globalization activists, such as the political maneuvering of nongovernmental agencies as they pressure globacracies. While I recognize that these political efforts are important, when I speak of "the movement" in this book, I speak mainly of the arm that plans and implements direct-action protests at summit and ministerial meetings.

In 2002 and 2003 I participated in five large anti-globalization protests, which included several sizable demonstrations at each of the following events: the WEF in New York City (February 2002); the G8 in Calgary and Ottawa, Canada (July 2002); the WB and IMF meeting in Washington, D.C. (September 2002); the WTO ministerial meeting in Cancun, Mexico (September 2003); and the FTAA meeting in Miami (November 2003). Because of the contentious nature of the movement, these locations were ideal for studying the social control of protests; for during the late 1990s, the movement emerged as one of the most common meeting places of control and resistance.

After the window breaking at the Battle of Seattle in 1999 and the killing of a young anarchist in the Genoa G8 protest in 2001, the anti-globalization movement began to receive increasing media attention, which often depicted it as dangerous and violent and a threat to public order.[1] Although unrelated, the 2001 terrorist attacks on the World Trade Center augmented the perceived threat of violence and public disorder. Since that time, anti-globalization protesters across the globe have been more likely to face highly orchestrated police responses to activists' dedicated use of direct action and social disruption. The years that I spent in the movement coincided with law enforcement's development and implementation of new techniques of control, which makes the anti-globalization movement empirically relevant to the study of social control.

Yet aspects of the movement make it problematic for study. In North America, large protest gatherings outside of global bureaucracies occur only two or three times per year. In other words, the field of study appears periodically, converging on a location and then disappearing until the next event. The field also changes city by city, each with a different context. Each time the movement emerges, a new set of circumstances appears along with a set of organizing web pages and e-mail lists that temporarily serve the movement. The fleeting, changeable nature of these protests makes research periodic, prolonged, and at times fragmented. With each event, the context changes slightly, as do police departments and local public attitudes. For this reason, I chronicle general tactics of social control rather than uncover universal laws. Taken together, the study of multiple sites offers a general overview of the possibilities of control and resistance.

BUILDING AN ORGANIC,
REFLEXIVE MODE OF INQUIRY

Before the WEF protest in New York, activists operated seven different listservs for that protest alone, each representing a different section of the movement. As that situation exemplifies, a fluid research approach is essential for entering, understanding, and experiencing this complicated field environment. Thus, I adopted a multifaceted ethnographic approach, which included field observations, interviews, and review of newspaper articles and police documents. Together, these methods wove together a story of how social control operates and affects those involved in dissent.

I collected most of my data during my years of participation in the movement. Early on, I adopted a combination of approaches: one methodological, the other ethical. The methodological side blends a grounded theoretical approach (Glaser and Strauss 1967) with a multi-sited ethnographic technique (Marcus 1995). The ethical approach derives from the sociological tradition of verstehen (Ferrell and Hamm 1998). Both grounded theory and multi-sited ethnography require the researcher to develop intimate knowledge of the environment under study. Following grounded theory, I allowed the issues to emerge organically, deriving them directly from my personal experience in the movement. From the start, my goal was to immerse myself in the protest, become a participant, and develop a theoretical understanding of the situation. While I recognized the impossibility of entering the field without preconceived notions, I did attempt to put aside all academic ideas and theories, hoping that a relatively clean slate would create room for a deep and rich experience as well as valuable insights.

Although the grounded approach was useful during the beginning stages of my research, it also had significant limitations. While the theory encourages organic, experienced-based research methods, it cannot deal coherently with the anti-globalization movement's shifting field environment. Rather, it clings to concepts of a static, geographically solid field that the researcher enters and observes. For this reason, the work of George Marcus (1995) is instructive. His notion of multi-sited ethnography recognizes the flexibility that contemporary ethnography needs to understand an increasingly complicated and interrelated world. Marcus argues that, until recently, the most common approach to ethnography was to focus on a single site and develop the systemic context around it. In contrast, he recommends "mov[ing] out from the single sites and local situations of conventional ethnographic research designs to examine the circulation of cultural meanings, objects, and identities in diffused time-space." This mode of ethnography recognizes the increasingly complicated relationship between time and space as experienced by contemporary subjectivities. It is mobile and flexible, offering a researcher the theoretical ability to explore "unexpected trajectories in tracing a cultural formation across and within multiple sites of activity that destabilizes the distinctions" (96). The researcher can examine the fluidity of a movement as it emerges, forms, and transforms in various geographical locations.

Even within this changing field, however, important social control themes cross each event. To fully grasp the meaning of control as it works on the minds and bodies of protesters, a researcher requires reflexivity, an approach that directly opposes positivism. At its most basic level, reflexivity is a researcher's ability to stand back and assess aspects of his or her own behavior, society, and culture in relation to factors such as motivation and meaning (Steier 1991). Regarding ethnography, reflexivity requires a researcher to deeply question objectivity—that is, the existence of a clean and unproblematic separation between the researcher and the researched. It involves understanding that, when researchers say something about their subjects, they say just as much about themselves. Rather than falling back on the positivistic idea that objective distance is needed to produce "truth," a reflexive approach embraces interaction and focuses on uncovering situated knowledge, encouraging participation and involvement with those under study in their own space and time (Burawoy 1998). Instead of adopting a stance of distance and objectivity, then, my methods deliberately blur the distinction between protester and researcher.

Finally, an important ethical dilemma guided my research methods: how could I research people who are running serious risks without exploiting their circumstances, without doing "drive-by research" or "airplane ethnography," in which researchers enter a setting, conduct studies, and then concern themselves primarily with publishing manuscripts for other researchers to read? I wanted the ethnography to have meaning beyond an academic exercise, both for me and for those in the movement. To solve this dilemma, I embraced the concept of *verstehen*, first introduced by Max Weber (Weber and Shils 1949) and later developed by other theorists (Ferrell and Hamm 1998). Verstehen is an approach to knowledge that calls for empathy, compassion, and understanding. A research method using verstehen necessarily involves a commitment to and involvement with those being studied as well as an attempt to connect oneself to the intentions and the context of their actions. Adopting this method involves opening oneself to the emotions, fears, and frustrations of those inside the movement; running alongside them in the streets; sleeping in the crowded meeting space; and directly experiencing the effects of social control on one's body and mind. From such direct experience, intimacy, connection, and solidarity with those in the movement, I developed many of my ideas about control.

THE DATA: PARTICIPATION, INTERVIEWS, AND DOCUMENTS

As I have described, my data for this book were collected during several years of participation in the anti-globalization movement. Fully immersing myself in the actions of each protest, I attended planning meetings (known as spokescouncils), participated in street marches and civil disobedience, blocked traffic, and observed police tactics from the protester side of the thin blue line. Placing myself in contentious (and at times dangerous) locations allowed me to experience firsthand the emotions, thoughts, and feelings produced by law enforcement's social control techniques. I deliberately blurred the boundary between observer and observed, hoping to induce in myself the fears and stresses that the police inflict on protesters as they employ the mechanisms of control. This approach worked well, producing intense emotions that fueled my analysis.

In addition, I supplemented my observations with fifteen semi-structured interviews with key protest organizers and fifteen semi-structured interviews with key police planners, for a total of thirty interviews. An important aspect in studying control and resistance is to understand what planners are thinking on each side of the police-protester divide. How does each side conceptualize what it is doing? How does each side view control and resistance? How do protesters think they are resisting? How do police view protesters? These questions guided my research.

I also reviewed newspaper articles and police documents. To help me understand how control operated through the media, I collected all available newspaper accounts five months before and three months after each protest—a total of 324 articles. I reviewed, coded, and analyzed all of them. The coding process started with the three general categories of social control outlined in the interview process (physical, legal, and psychological). I developed a coding scheme using a grounded theoretical approach. In addition, I collected police documents when they were available: police press releases, crowd control manuals, and after-event review reports. I used them to fill in the gaps on how police plan for and debrief after each protest.

WHAT IS GLOBALIZATION, AND WHY DO PEOPLE OPPOSE IT?

Scholars conjure up numerous terms to examine various social phenomena related to globalization, such as mass migration (Sassen 1998), the degradation of democracy (Brecher et al. 2000), the takeover of corporations (Starr 2000), environmental destruction (Beck 2000), global inequities (Bauman 1998), greater economic growth (Sachs 2000), and the rise of global networks (Castells 2000). Other scholars see such conceptions of globalization as academic trendiness (Nye 2001), arguing that it is neither unique nor new (Frank 1998). My aim here is not to focus on academic debates over globalization but to contextualize the anti-globalization movement by viewing the problems of corporate globalization critically in order to show why activists so strongly resist it. For heuristic purposes, we can divide globalization into three different areas of operation: cultural, economic, and political. While they work simultaneously and at times in conjunction, discussing them separately helps clarify how globalization affects people across the world.

Cultural Globalization

By cultural globalization, scholars generally mean the "movement of ideas, information, images, and people" (Keohane and Nye 2000, 116). In other words, it is the way in which information and cultural values spread from one area of the world to another (Appadurai 1996, 2001). Unfortunately, this movement takes place through corporate media and entertainment, meaning that cultural globalization imposes western values throughout the world.

This situation is not new. Individualism, science, objectivity, progress, secularism, and universal knowledge were central values in the European colonizations that began several centuries ago (Shiva 1997). Those values undermined and devalued indigenous knowledge, privileging western cosmological conceptions.

What is new today is the intensity and volume of the information flow. Through technology, western values advance secular philosophies entwined with neoliberalism and capitalism, thus transforming cultural beliefs throughout the world. From a critical perspective, then, cultural globalization is the homogenization of world cultures through goods such as movies, videos, music, and fast food. For this reason, corporate logos, such as McDonald's arches and Starbucks' signs, often become targets of the anti-globalization movement (Klein 2000).

Economic Globalization

The cultural sphere is closely related to the larger economic system, which is of great importance to the anti-globalization movement. In general, economic globalization, often called corporate globalization, refers to the expansion of economic markets across national boundaries. Trade barriers open so that goods, commodities, and finances can flow freely while human beings remain largely enclosed within national boundaries.

In a report for the International Forum on Globalization, a group of international scholars outlined the problems of economic globalization (Cavanagh et al. 2002). According to the report, economic globalization has four central tenets. First is an almost religious devotion to rapid, ever-increasing economic growth. Known as hypergrowth, this is an economic utopian ideal in which spiraling increases of production create enough wealth to solve all human needs and problems. Only through hypergrowth can the world's ailments be resolved: more production means more goods, and more goods means higher and better living standards. Fueling hypergrowth is a constant need for raw materials and cheap labor.

From the ideology of hypergrowth comes the argument for free trade, which involves breaking down trade tariffs that impede corporate expansion. Free trade removes all impediments to the flow of goods across national barriers. According to

Cavanagh and colleagues (2002), impediments to free trade usually come in the form of "environmental laws, public health
laws, food safety laws, laws pertaining to workers' rights and
opportunities, laws permitting nations to control investment on
their own soil, and laws attempting to retain national control
over local cultures" (20). Removing these so-called impediments has created grievances among anti-globalization activists
across the globe.

The second tenet of economic globalization is the privatization of public goods. Underlying the drive toward privatization
is the philosophy of competition. According to this perspective,
any economic endeavor not driven by an open, competitive
approach is doomed to fail. Implementing privatization requires
turning over public holdings to corporations so that they can be
run "more efficiently." But privatization policies have consequences—for instance, on the struggle over fresh water (Bello
and Mittal 2001). As Vandana Shiva (2002) sees it, water is the
ecological basis of all life and therefore is a public resource that
must be managed collectively among community members.
Taking a stance against economic globalization, she proposes
that water should remain part of the global commons and not be
turned into a private, corporate-owned commodity.

Unfortunately, developing nations, pressured by global
institutions and lack of funds, often decide to make water a
commodity; and water wars are the result. Bolivia is one example.
In 1999, the World Bank recommended that the Bolivian
government privatize the municipal waters of Cochabamba, a
semi-desert region. Following that recommendation, the
government put Cochabamba's water under the control of
International Water, a subsidiary of the American company
Bechtel (Barlow and Clarke 2002). Shortly thereafter, water
prices skyrocketed, rising to monthly payments of nearly 20
percent of an average family's yearly income. As a result,
the people of Cochabamba began a general protest against the

privatization of water, which led to the arrest and murder of local activists. After a period of serious contention, the people established a water democracy, taking back the water from corporations and the market. Such stories inspire the imaginations of activists across the globe. For example, the Pagan Cluster often uses the metaphor of water at anti-globalization protests. They put on a form of street theater known as "the flowing river," in which activists hold blue veils to imitate the flow of water. Between the veils are multiple forms of water life, such as fish, dolphins, and turtles.

Corporations argue that many services once performed by governments (such as public broadcasting, education, health, the police, and the military) need to be privatized to render them more efficient. The privatization of public goods is an important part of the ongoing negotiations in the FTAA and the WTO, and activists often focus on the issue during protests. In addition, privatization has extended its reach beyond commodification to the colonization of knowledge and the control of biological cycles (see Chapter 2). Shiva (1997) describes how corporations use trade-related intellectual property rights (TRIPS) to pirate indigenous knowledge. Calling the process *biopiracy*, she describes how corporations, enforced by globacracies, use TRIPS to steal and form monopolies on local indigenous knowledge of plants and medicines. To illustrate, Shiva offers the example of neem, a native tree in India used for centuries by indigenous people as a natural pesticide and a medicine. Because of TRIPS, several corporations now own patents on a chemical composition derived from neem, in essence taking knowledge that developed through community-based, collective processes and calling it their own. Ignoring indigenous knowledge is a legacy of colonial thinking that is enforced through global institutions.

Similarly, corporations use biotechnology to infiltrate the biological life cycle (Fowler 1995, Shiva 1995). Several corporations, including Monsanto, are genetically manipulating plant and animal species to make them more "efficient" and profitable. Monsanto, for example, has introduced terminator technology: the genetic reengineering of the plant life cycle so that a seed can only reproduce once. As a consequence, farmers must buy the high-yielding seed every year, making them dependent on the corporation for sustenance. These issues have influenced the symbolism displayed in various anti-globalization protests, including the seed, earth, and plant themes at the Cancun WTO protest.

The third tenet of globalization is the development of export-oriented trade and investment. Economic globalization favors the lifting of barriers and trade tariffs so that investment can flow freely across borders (Cavanagh et al. 2002). With investment comes efficiency and profit, or so the theory goes. According to Nobel Prize–winning economist Joseph Stiglitz (2002), the theory beneath globalization is the concept of comparative advantage, which posits that the liberalization of global trade will encourage investment capital to flow to areas where labor and resources are cheap. In this utopian vision, all nations benefit (eventually) from the lifting of barriers because the "invisible hand" guides the market toward efficiency.

Yet when globacracies actually apply comparative advantage, the outcome is not always beneficial. With the development of export-oriented production, local economies of production are devalued, discouraged, and sometimes eliminated. For instance, small farmers are lost in the push for larger global agricultural production. As a result, such policies have inspired farmers and their supporters to become leaders of the international resistance to globalization (Cavanagh et al. 2002).

Political Globalization

Contrary to common belief, economic globalization is not happening naturally. Rather, it has been implemented through various global economic institutions, such at the WTO, the IMF, and the WB, and through multinational agreements such as the FTAA. The crafting and regulation of these policies constitute political globalization. The organizations just mentioned facilitate corporate access to economies around the world, helping companies capture markets by forcing deregulation or eliminating national laws that inhibit foreign investment. Structural adjustment loans, popular in the 1980s and 1990s, are example of policies driven mainly by the ideology of privatization, liberalization, and fiscal austerity. In *Globalization and Its Discontents*, Joseph Stiglitz (2002) describes how the WB, with the encouragement of the IMF, placed strict conditions on nations that were seeking loans to survive financial crisis. The structural adjustment conditions required nations to privatize public resources, downsize civil service employment, lift laws protecting local industries, and devalue currency. As a result, structural adjustment produced severe levels of impoverishment in the developing world; and fifty-six IMF riots or austerity protests, "including demonstrations, strikes and riots, were waged in Latin America, the Caribbean, the Middle East, Africa and Eastern Europe. In the 1990s, protests defending social welfare policies erupted in Western Europe and Canada" (Starr 2000, 46). These structural adjustment policies resulted in an external debt crisis that has threatened the stability of entire nations, as in Argentina in 2001.

The globacracy known as the IMF is dedicated to fostering the philosophies of economic globalization. Created after World War II, its original mission was to implement measures to ensure the stability of the international financial system, steering the global economy away from the possibility of another Great Depression. By the 1980s, however, the organization had assumed a different role. Abandoning Keynesian policies and adopting a neoliberal philosophy (liberalization, deregulation, and privatization), the IMF began pushing strongly for the deregulation of cross-border trade and financial flows (Stiglitz 2002). This deregulation, which included the elimination of trade barriers, created an initial burst of economic investment from the industrial world to developing nations. Yet these policies also produced what Robert J. Shiller (2001) calls irrational exuberance, with negative consequences such as real estate and stock market bubbles. Working with the WB and structural adjustment loans, the IMF implemented policies that resulted in mass debt crises in several nations, including Mexico, Argentina, Brazil, and several Asian countries (Bello and Mittal 2001, Cavanagh et al. 2002, Stiglitz 2002). The bursting of this artificial economic bubble was the catalyst for wide grassroots dissatisfaction with globalization and the institutions that support it.

The WTO is another pillar of economic globalization. Originally, it grew out of the General Agreement of Tariffs and Trade (GATT), which was created after World War II to reduce tariffs in goods and services and to set broad trade principles. GATTs work in negotiation rounds that can last for several years. In the 1980s, fueled by the Reagan and Thatcher administrations, a drastically different round of negotiations began. This time, the goals were to "expand the GATT disciplines to bind signatory governments to a set of multilateral policies regarding the service, government procurement, and investment sectors; to establish global limits on government regulation of environmental, food safety, and products standards; to establish new protections for corporate intellectual property rights granted in rich countries; and to have this broad panoply of one-size-fits-all rules strongly enforced over every level of government in every signatory country" (Cavanagh et al. 2002, 44).

Pushed primarily by multinational corporations, this round of negotiations (called the Uruguay Round) ended in 1994 with the formation of the WTO, which adopted the role of enforcer. Composed of trade ministers from participating nations, the organization had the authority to regulate trade using commanding and unprecedented built-in powers. For instance, WTO courts regulate and enforce trade agreements. If a nation does not comply, the entire country can be brought to court, where WTO judges make rulings on disputes. In short, the WTO is the power mechanism that enforces the policy agenda of the IMF and WB.

At least two other organizations also affect globalization: the WEF and the G8. According to its website, the "World Economic Forum is an independent international organization committed to improving the state of the world. The Forum provides a collaborative framework for the world's leaders to address global issues, engaging particularly its corporate members in global citizenship" (World Economic Forum 2004). Since 1971, the WEF has held an annual meeting of chief executives from the world's richest corporations, national political leaders (presidents, prime ministers, and others), and selected intellectuals and journalists, usually in Davos, Switzerland. Today these meetings include more than 2,000 people each year. Thus, even though it is not tied to a political or national interest, the WEF provides space for the global elite to meet, greet, and network. As François Houtart and François Polet (2001) note, the WEF represents globalization from above.

The Group of 8 represents the eight most powerful economies in the developed world: the United States, the United Kingdom, Canada, France, Russia, Italy, Germany, and Japan. Although it meets annually, the G8 is an informal, non-legalized international institution that relies on a regular leadership summit rather than a formal international bureaucracy (Kirton 2004). It serves two general functions. First, it provides an important "agenda setting function, for participating and outside governments, as it creates action-forcing deadlines in the preparatory process, generates initiatives, and induces governments to create, confirm or revise their positions on the issues the Summit highlights" (7). Second, G8 members operate as authoritative decision makers, a sort of directorate of global governance. In their meetings, they discuss global security issues as well as coming global trade negotiations. "[This] decisional function includes the particular case of 'money mandated' to fulfill particular functions, casting the G8 in the role of providing the discretionary budget for global governance, on the expenditure if not the revenue side" (8). In short, the G8 is a steering committee for globalization.

WHICH ANTI-GLOBALIZATION MOVEMENT?

Social movement scholars believe that a set of grievances is a necessary but not sufficient condition for mobilization (Tarrow 1989). Yet prolonged mobilization efforts without grievances are unlikely. In the case of the anti-globalization movement, the negative consequences of structural adjustments, privatization, and deregulation provided the necessary grievances; and in the 1990s, movements from all over the world began to focus on globalization and neoliberalism as root causes of their problems.

In addition to clearly articulating grievances, movements need to make their grievances visible. This process is connected to what Don Mitchell (2003) describes as a problem of representation: where do protesters gather to publicize their grievances? All social movements must answer this question in one way or another if they wish to make the public aware of their grievances.

The case becomes more complicated when we consider the difficulty of making abstract grievances visible and comprehensible, but movements must solve this problem to reach mass audiences. For example, the civil rights movement named racism, segregation, and voting rights as its primary grievances. Activists solved the representation problem by identifying segregated stores, courthouses, schools, and voting registrations as locations for struggle. In other words, they publicized their grievances by targeting these spaces and showing how violence was required to maintain segregation. Their cause became visible as authorities jailed, beat, and harassed them. A similar process occurred in the anti-globalization movement.

According to many movement activists, economic globalization is a major cause of global problems, and globacracies force economic globalization. Thus, it should come as no surprise to learn that, starting in the late 1990s, the anti-globalization movement coalesced around WB, IMF, WTO, WEF, and G8 meetings as locations of protest. Scholars and activists often refer to the movement as the "movement of movements" because its grievances are vast and widespread (Mertes 2004). Therefore, before undertaking an analysis of social control, we need to understand the movement's organizational structure as it plans for protest.

Anarchism and Direct Action

Although diverse groups gather at these protests, anarchism is a basic common philosophy of the movement. To the layperson (and the media), *anarchy* means chaos, or the unruly behavior of humans outside the restriction of the law. Heavily influenced by the work of Thomas Hobbes (1991), this view depicts humans as essentially selfish, motivated mainly by self-interest. Accordingly, human nature requires a social contract, a set of rules that will protect us from each other. The government, or the sovereign, becomes the entrusted protector and executioner of these rules.

Anarchist theorists paint a different picture of human nature. Instead of situating selfishness within the human subject, anarchist thought views the state as the root of evil (Goldman and Drinnon 1969; Berkman 1971, 2003): "[the government] fills the world with violence, with fraud and deceit, with oppression and misery" (Berkman 1971, 27). For anarchists,

humans are inherently cooperative; they value freedom, autonomy, and self-rule above all else.

In this view, anarchists work toward two general goals. First,
they want to dismantle oppressive, hierarchical institutions.
Second, they want to replace those institutions with organic,
horizontal, and cooperative versions based on autonomy, solidarity, voluntary association, mutual aid, and direct action.
While the anti-globalization movement is not always explicitly
anarchist, the parts that I study do hold autonomy, voluntary
association, and mutual aid as central values, as is apparent in the
basic organizational style of the movement (discussed more fully
later in this chapter). During a protest, for instance, it adopts a
diversity of tactics: an agreement that no one ideology governs
the actions of people in the streets. To ensure solidarity, activists
are asked to respect and not publicly criticize protesters
who choose tactics different from their own. Autonomy and
solidarity, rather than coordination and hierarchy, are guiding
principles.

Consistent with notions of voluntary association, activists
also negotiate and develop agreements on how to work together
in the streets. For example, during the Seattle WTO protests in
1999, groups negotiated and signed a common agreement
before the protest. Participating groups and individuals freely
agreed "to refrain from violence, physical or verbal; not to carry
weapons; not to bring or use illegal drugs or alcohol; and not to
destroy property" (Starhawk 2002a, 53). This agreement was
only temporary, not a lifetime commitment to a philosophical
position. At other gatherings such agreements were more difficult to negotiate, resulting in conflict and a lack of unity.
Nevertheless, in all the protests that I attended I noted a common respect for the notions of autonomy, voluntary association,
and mutual agreement.

Direct action, or taking action based on one's beliefs, is also
important in the anti-globalization movement. Direct action

differs significantly from symbolic action. For example, for a group working against neighborhood gentrification, direct action might mean squatting in an abandoned building to fight development. For a group working to end homelessness, it might mean cooking and serving a meal for homeless people. In contrast, symbolic action might involve lobbying an authority in an attempt to change policy. Working in the anarchist tradition, direct action does not require an appeal to authority. Rather, it means solving the problem concretely and directly confronting authority if necessary.

Direct action is often confused with civil disobedience. Generally speaking, civil disobedience involves violating an immoral law, possibly in order to challenge it through the court system. Participants often plan to get arrested in service of a larger cause. The anti-nuclear movement, for instance, used civil disobedience along with nonviolent tactics such as passive resistance (such as "going limp") when police employed force. Direct action differs slightly in that participants choose disruptive tactics without anticipating or seeking arrest. To some, it also means resisting and challenging police and state authority as well as protesting injustice.

In a protest, direct action might take the form of a rent strike, a consumer boycott, or a blockade; it may involve sit-ins, squatting, tree living, or the occupation of target buildings. In short, direct action disrupts and confronts rather than negotiates. Yet contrary to common perception, it is not inherently violent and, as a tactic, has been used by peace and civil rights movements from the 1930s through the 1970s (Tracy 1996).

The anti-globalization movement's dedication to direct action means that it sometimes rejects cooperation with authorities when planning a protest. In such cases, organizers do not seek marching and protest permits, respect protest zones, or negotiate with police before an action. Protesters may destroy property, usually targeted corporate symbols such as Starbucks, Pizza Hut,

3-1. Mexican university students engage in direct action by blocking traffic in Cancun for three hours, directly outside of the conference center where the WTO is meeting. (Photograph by Luis Fernandez and Sue Hilderbrand)

or Citibank. Property destruction may also involve tearing down fences erected to protect meeting areas. Nevertheless, while I have seen human–on–human violence at anti-globalization protests, in my experience it is usually administered by the police, not the other way around.

The Affinity Group Model

The affinity group is the basic organizational unit of the anti-globalization movement, and that model's inherent qualities are directly linked to the way in which the state polices the movement. Affinity groups are small, self-sufficient groups of individuals who know and trust each other. Ideally, each group includes five to twenty people, few enough to make effective collective decision making possible. Working autonomously, the groups decide what level of risk to take and what types of action to pursue, ranging from marching in a protest to direct action and civil disobedience. Affinity groups may work individually or join other affinity groups to form larger clusters that plan and implement collective action. Some affinity groups exist for long periods of time; others form and dissolve within the period of a single protest.

The affinity group model first appeared in Spain the latter part of the nineteenth century, when small groups of radicals gathered to discuss and plan actions based on the principles of autonomy and mutual aid (Bookchin 1977). By 1910, Spanish workers had formed a network called the Confederacion Nacional del Trabajo (the National Confederation of Labor), organized primarily around the affinity group model, in which individual groups retained their independent nature. Relevant to today's anti-globalization movement, the Spanish workers formed these groups primarily on the basis of locality (Bookchin 1977).[2] By 1927, the Federacion Anarquista Iberica (the Iberian Anarchist Federation) organized local, regional, and national councils using the affinity group model.[3] The federation grew to more than 50,000 members, all coordinated by committees of delegates from affinity groups. But unlike organizations such as labor unions, local affinity groups remained autonomous, retaining decision-making powers over educational and political programs. Due to the small size of each group, infiltration of the movement was kept at a minimum: unknown members were not admitted.

The model came to the United States in 1977, when activists, organized in affinity groups, took over a nuclear power plant in Seabrook, New Hampshire (Notes from Nowhere 2003). By the time the anti-globalization movement adopted it, this type of organizing had been used in North America for several years. The movement's most notorious, and successful, use of the model occurred during the 1999 WTO protest in Seattle. Some 50,000 activists gathered in Seattle, mostly organized in affinity groups that performed various functions, such as preparing food, conducting direct action training, and organizing street theater. Some groups were there as support, while others participated in direct action (Starhawk 2002b). The affinity group approach (aided by several labor union members) caught the Seattle police off guard. They were unprepared for the level of coordinated action that could result from such a loose organizational form, and activists succeeded in completely shutting down the WTO meetings. Even more successful was their ability to place the movement and its grievances in newspaper and television headlines around the globe.

In my experience, affinity groups in the anti-globalization movement vary in size, intensity, and commitment. As mentioned, some affinity groups remain together for several years; others assemble months before an action; a few form during an action and disband immediately after it. But these last groups are rare and tend to play a less important role in organizing and participating in direct action, probably because the level of trust among individuals is lower than it is in longer-standing groups.

A movement built around the affinity group model is difficult to defuse because it has no real center or central figure. Affinity groups are like singularities within the multitude. Once linked, they can swarm around cities, popping up in unexpected places and dissolving by the time the police arrive. To adapt, police must use control mechanisms that go beyond physical repression to include the manipulation of space, as I will show in the following chapters. The affinity group model also makes police infiltration more difficult. They have to shift their intelligence gathering to spokescouncil meetings and surveillance of web pages and Internet discussion groups.

Yet despite these advantages for the movement, the affinity group model can have negative consequences for protesters: it makes participation more difficult for individuals who don't belong to an affinity group. This was my experience when I attended my first anti-globalization protest. As a novice, I was unclear about proper movement etiquette. At first, my plan was to enter the movement as a street medic.[4] I learned, however, that street medic affinity groups were some of the most insular in the movement: medics need to trust each other implicitly when dealing with stressful and potentially threatening situations. Although other groups were more willing to accept individuals, I found that, for the most part, attending a protest as an individual was difficult. I am sure that other would-be protesters felt similar frustrations.

To some degree, such difficulties are intentional. One organizer told me that the movement discouraged "summit hopping"—the tendency for individual activists to jump from one globalization summit to another, turning the movement into a form of activist tourism. Rather, the movement wanted the individuals who attended a protest to be part of ongoing community work. In the long run, however, such an attitude may prove detrimental: a movement grows as it incorporates people who at first do not fully grasp its ideology or tactics.

Clusters

A cluster is an association of multiple affinity groups that come together to work on a given task or as part of a larger action.[5] Because affinity groups are relatively small, a collaboration of groups facilitates larger work, such as a street performance or a blockade. Clusters take on different types of actions depending on movement needs and a mutual agreement regarding the level of risk a particular cluster is willing to endure. For example, a cluster might agree to block an intersection or a section of town (as the Pagan Cluster did in Washington, D.C.), cook and serve food for activists, or organize a communication system.

Clusters organize according to various criteria. Members may be united by region (the California Cluster), issue (environmentalism), action (direct action or civil disobedience), or willing level of risk (Rant Collective 2004). Like affinity groups, clusters can form and disband in one day, organize over multiple days, or exist for several years. For example, the Pagan Cluster is a long-lasting cluster that has participated at multiple protests. Pagan affinity groups exist throughout North America. Generally speaking, modern paganism includes polytheism and a strong connection with nature, although specific meanings are difficult to pin down. Not all pagans are activists, of course, but those who participate in the anti-globalization use magic and earth symbols as part of their repertoire of contention. Each protest I attended had an active Pagan Cluster, varying in size from protest to protest. In Cancun, there were approximately forty pagans; in Miami, there were more than 150.

There are other clusters in the movement as well, such as the Black Block (a cluster of anarchist affinity groups) and the Green Block (an ecology-based cluster). Names vary depending on activists' creativity or a protest's specific need. The Black Block is a consistent presence, developing when anarchist affinity groups gather at an action. The cluster is distinguished by an openness to police confrontation, blockades, and property

3-2. Pagans perform a ritual during the 2002 "People's Strike" protest at Dupont Circle in Washington, D.C. (Photograph by Luis Fernandez and Sue Hilderbrand)

destruction. They wear black clothing and cover their faces with bandanas. Adopted by North American anarchists in the late 1990s, this tactic developed in the 1980s in the European autonomous movement to make police surveillance and control more difficult (Katsiaficas 1997). Since then, the Black Block has been common at anti–globalization protests and is a common police excuse for targeting the movement.

Spokescouncils

The movement uses a spokescouncil to coordinate mass actions that involve multiple affinity groups in several clusters. The concept is simple. Each affinity group or cluster selects a "spoke," or representative, to attend the spokescouncil meeting. Each spoke is empowered to make decisions for the affinity group. At the meeting, spokes discuss pertinent issues and collectively decide on current or future protest actions.

Spokescouncil meetings start several days before a protest, about the time when activists arrive in the city hosting the protest. Meetings occur every night until the final protest event. At the protests I attended, meeting attendees varied from 100 to 350 activists. All decisions are made by consensus. At the beginning of each session, the group selects a facilitator, a notetaker, and a stacker to run the meeting. The facilitator helps the group create an agenda and then guides participants through it; the note taker records decisions; the stacker keeps track of those interested in talking during the meeting, who indicate their interest by raising their hands.

The level of organization at a spokescouncil varies from protest to protest. Depending on local activists' experience, some meetings have effective facilitators; others do not. At some protests, spokescouncils consist mainly of spoke representatives; at others they consist mostly of individuals representing themselves. Some of the meetings I attended were long, exhausting, and inefficient. Nevertheless, the structure supports the values of nonhierarchical organizing.

Spokescouncil meetings serve the movement in several ways. First, they are introductory and informative seminars on what local activists are planning. For example, when I first entered the movement, a spokescouncil meeting provided some basic information about the protest week, such as the starting times of marches. Second, the meetings work as informal networks in which newly arrived affinity groups can get information about emerging clusters. At several meetings, I heard announcements such as "We are planning an action that has a potential for arrest. We need affinity groups that can run this risk. If interested, please talk to me"; and "We are an affinity group planning actions, and we need legal advice. If you are with the legal team, please come talk to us."[6] Third, the meetings are decision-making bodies in which activists collectively plan spontaneous and creative protest activities. For example, during the 2003 IMF/WB protest in Washington, D.C., activists used the spokescouncil to plan what they called "The People's Strike." The goal was to shut down the entire city. To coordinate the effort, activists divided the city into approximately ten areas and asked each cluster and affinity group to select an area. There was little discussion about what those individual groups planned to do. In other words, the spokescouncil facilitated the process of organizing without directly governing which actions would happen where.

The spokescouncil approach confirms the movement's belief in mutual aid, collective decision making, and nonhierarchical leadership. Yet it also has limitations. In the hands of an inexperienced facilitator, a spokescouncil meeting can be dull and exhausting. For instance, during the IMF/WB protest in Washington, D.C., I attended a meeting facilitated by a young, inexperienced group of activists charged with organizing a large mass action that required complicated logistics. The activists could not solve basic organizational problems, such as delegating work for a communication system during the large day of action.

Spokescouncil meetings also tend to be long. In New York City, I attended meetings that lasted for more than five hours, continuing late into the night and leaving activists exhausted for the next day's action, which started at 6:30 A.M. Some meetings are disorganized, leading to general confusion over the starting time, the location of events, or the nature of the protest. According to Judy, an experienced activist in the movement, "This is the price we sometimes pay for true democracy."

Finally, spokescouncil meetings are easily subject to police infiltration. While activists always ask journalists and law enforcement agents to identify themselves and leave the room, there is ample evidence (as discussed in Chapter 6) that police take advantage of the meetings to collect information on movement activities. Given that affinity groups are difficult to infiltrate, these meetings are the logical space for surveillance.

Sections of the Movement

Given globalization's international nature, it is not surprising that a wide variety of groups from all over the world attend summit and ministerial protests. They range from the affinity groups just described, to transnational nongovernmental organizations, to unions and indigenous people. All of these groups must share the protest space, work out agreements on street behavior, and coordinate large marches. This work is not easy and is riddled with problems.

In the weeks leading to a protest, various groups organize panels, discussions, forums, trainings, and teach-ins. Depending on the summit or ministerial agenda, topics may include deforestation, direct action training, water privatization, bioengineering, or agriculture, among many others. For example, at the 2003 WTO meetings in Cancun, an International Forum on Globalization included international activist-scholars who were discussing the plight of small farmers across the world, in keeping with the ministerial agenda of opening up agricultural markets. Simultaneously, the Union Nacional de Organizaciones Regionales de Campesinos Autonomous, together with indigenous people and farmers from all over the world, held a *foro campesino* (farmers' forum) where farmers could discuss food sovereignty issues. In New York, Columbia University students organized a teach-in called "Globalizing Social Justice: A Counter Summit to the World Economic Forum," which offered street medic and direct action training. Thus, the weeks before a protest are packed with an exciting array of planning and education activities. Some are formally recognized by official institutions such as the United Nations. Others are more informal, linked to direct action and street protest.

To support street actions, activists create several distinct spaces to provide protesters with information, media access, first aid, and legal help. An essential part of protests is the convergence center, a physical location in which activists share information about the coming protests. At least one volunteer is present to provide basic information, such as city maps or public transportation schedules. The center also has community message boards, lists of planned activities, and schedules of ongoing forums and panels. For arriving affinity groups, the convergence center is the place to find the time and location of spokescouncil meetings as well as information about which clusters need volunteers—in other words, to give and receive the vital information required for mobilization. As such, it is an easy target for police harassment and surveillance.

The independent media center (IMC) is another activist-created work space. Activists build an IMC at each meeting, providing access to computers, video and sound editors, fax machines, and Internet connections. Participants from all over the world can record, edit, and update web pages to keep their comrades and the public informed about the protest. Each IMC is part of the larger global phenomenon of Indymedia, an Internet-based network of IMCs that has developed since the 1999 WTO protests in Seattle (Atton 2003). Consisting mainly of web space for local activists, Indymedia spans the globe, including almost every major city in the United States and Europe as well as areas of Latin America, Oceania, Africa, and Asia.

In the anarchist tradition, Indymedia tries to dismantle hierarchical institutions and build new participatory models of organization. In this instance, the target institution is the corporate media. The basic idea behind Indymedia is to *become* the media. Rather than relying on how the corporate media cover a protest, Indymedia makes reporters out of protesters, allowing activists to disseminate their own information and provide a view of the protest that may be very different from the mainstream media's. During recent protests, IMC activists even created and disseminated laminated cards proclaiming activists to be members of the press and thus eligible for access to formal summit programs.

In addition to a convergence center and an IMC, all protests have a street medic center or a first aid house. Street medics are a collection of doctors, nurses, emergency medical technicians, herbalists, and other trained individuals. Their presence has become standard at protests since the 1999 Battle of Seattle, when police used tear gas, pepper spray, and other "nonlethal" weapons to subdue activists. Because police usually do not allow professional medical teams (such as ambulances) beyond police lines, street medics are often the only alternative for an injured protester.

Street medics use the affinity group model to organize their activities, usually forming in the activists' hometown and arriving at the protest as a tight, trusting, and insulated cell. For example, the Black Cross Health Collective is an affinity group of street medics from Portland, Oregon. Founded shortly after the WTO protests in Seattle, the group provides free care to the radical community at progressive actions, such as anti-war or anti-globalization protests. In addition, the collective trains radicals to keep themselves safe in the street (Black Cross Health Collective 2004). Members have offered such training in Los Angeles; Vancouver, B.C.; Seattle; Olympia; and Portland. In addition, the group has conducted pharmaceutical trials, looking for ways to neutralize pepper spray with a mixture that relieves pain when applied directly to the eyes.

The Black Cross Health Collective (2004) has explicit political aims: "We believe that health care is political. The kind of care we do or don't receive, where and how we receive that care, who provides that care, who has access to training to provide care, and what kinds of training are smiled or frowned upon, all involve inherently political issues. We believe that systems need to be changed. . . the health care system right along with all others." Like other segments of the movement, the organization is partly based on an anarchist model—voluntary, nonhierarchical, and autonomous. It is also critical of larger institutions, such as corporate health care. At the same time, it seeks to create its own solutions by providing its own care.

Finally, protests host legal teams or legal observers: activists with basic legal training who watch and record the actions of all law enforcement officers at demonstrations. Their primary purpose is to discourage police attacks on demonstrators by training activists to record police misconduct. In addition, they collect information that might be useful in criminal defense cases against demonstrators or for legal challenges or class-action lawsuits launched against the police or other government agencies after a protest. Working in pairs, legal observers use a variety of techniques to record information, including still and video cameras and note taking.

The Impact of September 11, 2001

Although the 1999 WTO protest did not start the anti-globalization movement, it did spark an intense series of global protests (Ayres 2004) targeting globacracies. In 2000 and 2001, there were thirteen large anti-globalization protests worldwide, including the IMF/WB protests in Washington, D.C., where thousands of protesters tried to shut down the meetings, leading to six hundred "preemptive" arrests; the WEF protests in Melbourne; the G20 meetings in Montreal; the Summit of the Americas protest in Quebec City; and the G8 summit in Genoa, where the movement suffered its first human casualty. These mobilizations did not occur in a vacuum but amid hundreds of ongoing local protests in developed and developing nations.

Between 1999 and 2001, the movement gained momentum rapidly, increasing its number of participating activists and winning several victories. In the United States, the movement felt strong, confident, and confrontational; anti-globalization activists were willing to take risks not seen in decades. But the terrorist attacks on New York's World Trade Center on September 11, 2001, drastically changed the context surrounding the movement and the risk to protesters.

Those attacks had an immediate effect on the movement. For starters, an anti-globalization protest planned for September 29, 2001, in Washington, D.C., was canceled by organizers. A few months later, during the World Economic Summit protest in New York City, the memory of the attacks was so powerful that protesters and the public seemed to have little tolerance for mass disruption. At the very least, the attacks temporarily dampened activists' enthusiasm for confrontational tactics.

In addition, U.S. authorities embraced more aggressive policing approaches, indicating an increased lack of tolerance for dissent and demonstrating "forcefully the continued relevance of the state in the structuring of movement activity" (Ayres 2004, 25). While there is evidence that the police were already adopting coercive methods of policing before September 11 (della Porta and Tarrow 2001, Steward 2001), the intensity increased dramatically after the attacks. Passing of the USA PATRIOT Act in October 2001 made it easier for U.S. policing agencies to criminalize dissent (Chang 2002). At the very least, the attacks and the USA PATRIOT Act allowed the police to equate, if only temporarily, anti-globalization activists with terrorists, making mobilization more difficult.

The rebirth of a strong, if momentary, anti-war movement before the war in Iraq also affected the movement. At first, activists tried to connect the war and globalization, arguing that the war was a form of military globalization backed by corporations who benefit from military contracts.[7] But although the anti-war movement subsided after the Iraq invasion, the anti-globalization movement has continued to organize against global institutions, leading some scholars to conclude that the movement will persist into the future (Buttel and Gould 2004). And the evidence supports these conclusions. For instance, tens of thousands of people protested the G8 meetings in Germany in June 2007.

All of the protest events I participated in for this book occurred after September 11, 2001. While it is still too early to tell, these protests may represent the downward trend in the larger protest cycle of the movement in North America. Nevertheless, they are important in the study of social control, given the increasing police presence resulting from "the war on terror," the terrorism laws applied to dissenters, and the public perception of protest.

CHAPTER 4

Managing and Regulating Protest

SOCIAL CONTROL AND THE LAW

IN NOVEMBER 2004, the Free Trade Area of the Americas (FTAA) met in Miami. Representing thirty-four countries from the Americas, national trade ministers negotiated to eliminate trade and investment barriers on virtually all goods and services provided anywhere between Canada and Tierra del Fuego. Thousands of protesters also traveled to Miami to express dissent, arguing that such an agreement was undemocratic, undermined labor and environmental laws, moved to privatize vital public services, and would likely benefit corporations more than ordinary people.

Implementing the now infamous "Miami model," the Miami-Dade Police Department, in collaboration with dozens of local, state, and national law enforcement agencies, welcomed protesters with decisive force. In the days before the protest, the police patrolled the streets with heavily armored, military-style personnel carriers and swept over downtown Miami with police helicopters. By demonstration time, the city was packed with thousands of police officers dressed like soldiers in khaki uniforms with full black body armor and gas masks, marching down the streets shouting, "Back! . . . back!" while beating batons against their shields. For no apparent reason, they fired skin-piercing rubber bullets indiscriminately into crowds of unarmed

4-1. Four deep and dressed in full riot gear, Miami officers surround protesters during the 2003 FTAA protest. (Photograph by Seth Paine)

peaceful protesters, sprayed tear gas at thousands of others, and shocked still others with tasers. It is no hyperbole to say that, during the FTAA demonstration, Miami became a militarized sector, closely resembling a war zone.

The growth and normalization of police paramilitarism has been well documented in the criminology literature (Kraska 1997, 2001). What differed in this case was law enforcement's use of sophisticated military equipment and tactics in the policing of dissent. But to fully grasp what happened in Miami and how the social control of dissent operates, we must look beyond the evidence of direct repression. Although disturbing and at times unbelievable, such repression is a visible part of the state's repertoire of control. But the state exerts less obvious control as well. Behind the scenes, and for months before a protest, it engages in legal tactical maneuvering in hopes of changing the demonstration's nature and inhibiting its scope. This chapter examines the legal strategies that police employ to regulate,

manage, and pacify dissent: city ordinances and codes as well as
zoning restrictions and demonstration permits that constrain the
actions available to protesters.

CITY ORDINANCES

Two months before the FTAA meetings, the Miami City
Commission began considering a revision to its Streets and
Sidewalks Ordinance that would specifically target anti-
globalization protesters.[1] The first draft of the revised ordinance
was submitted to the commission on September 11, 2003 (perhaps to associate it with the idea of protecting Miami from terrorists). The ordinance's purpose was clearly stated at a
commission hearing on October 23, 2003: "to establish reasonable time, place and manner regulations concerning materials
and objects that may be possessed, carried or used by those participating in parades and public assembly." Alluding to past
instances of "significant personal injuries and property damage"
and "potential . . . civil disturbance and unrest during certain
upcoming events," the revised ordinance sought to create new
and specific regulations concerning parades, demonstrations, rallies, and assemblies, redefining *parades* and *assemblies* as follows:

> The term "parade" shall mean any march, demonstration,
> procession, motorcade, or promenade consisting of persons,
> animals, or vehicles, or a combination thereof, having a
> common purpose, design, destination, or goal; upon any
> public place, which parade, march, demonstration, proces-
> sion, motorcade, or promenade does not comply with nor-
> mal and usual traffic regulations or control.
>
> The term "assembly" shall mean any meeting, demon-
> stration, picket line, rally, gathering, or group of three (3) or
> more persons, animals, or vehicles, or a combination
> thereof, having a common purpose, design, or goal, upon
> any public street, sidewalk, alley, park, or other public place,
> which assembly substantially inhibits the usual flow of

pedestrian or vehicular travel or which occupies any public area, other than a parade, as defined above. (City of Miami, September 25, 2003, sec. 54-6.1[a])

The ordinance also forbade any person to wear a gas mask that "would protect the respiratory tract and face against irritation, noxious or poisonous gases" (sec. 54-6.1[b]) as well as bullet-proof vests or body armor. Clearly, the ordinance was aimed specifically at the FTAA protests: as first written, it expired on November 27, a few days after the departure of the FTAA delegates.

The proposed ordinance outraged activists organizing in Miami. Mobilizing quickly, they sent out national bulletins, via activist e-mail lists, asking people to contact city commissioners and urge them to vote against the ordinance. The result was thousands of phone calls and e-mails to the city of Miami. In addition, unions and nongovernmental agencies pressured local politicians, asking them to reconsider. The American Civil Liberties Union (2003) quickly came out against the ordinance because it "criminalizes objects instead of actions." As a result, the city commission postponed the voting date for the ordinance and asked staff members to rewrite questionable sections.

On October 15, 2003, the commission received an alternative copy of the protest law and passed it with changes. Gone from this draft were the sections banning gas masks and bullet-proof vests, and the law no longer expired after the FTAA meetings. Yet it was still illegal for protesters to carry ordinary objects that could be used for "violent purposes." Outlawed were any signs or posters not made "solely of a cloth, paper, flexible or cardboard material no greater then one-quarter inch in thickness." Also banned were sticks, pointed objects, balloons (not filled with air), scissors, spray paint, glass containers, or any object that could "potentially" turn into a projectile. The city commission outlawed "anything hard that may be thrown and is carried with the intent to use unlawfully," giving the police full authority to define what constitutes "hard" or "intent to use unlawfully." Finally, they declared illegal any "coordinated movement" of two or more people with the intent of gaining public attention that interferes with the normal flow of traffic. With the passing of this ordinance, a "public assembly" of eight people or more would be illegal if they gathered, peacefully or otherwise, for more than thirty minutes (sec. 54-6.1[b]).

The Miami City Commission passed the ordinance four days before the FTAA protest, enough time for the law to take effect but not for movement lawyers to challenge it. When protesters hit the Miami streets in mid-November, the law was fully operative; and months later, city commissioners openly admitted its purpose to journalists. "We would be kidding ourselves if we said that without the [FTAA meetings] this law would have been passed," said Tomas Regalado, the commissioner responsible for putting forth the ordinance (Salazar 2004, B2). On March 11, approximately three months after the FTAA had meetings ended, the commission voted to rescind the ordinance.

Miami is not the only city that has used ordinances to regulate and control dissent and protest. For example, Savannah, Georgia, adopted a similar ordinance to police protest at the G8 summit in April 2004. The language in the Miami and Savannah ordinances was almost identical. These temporary ordinances constitute a new type of legal control, one absent from previous anti-globalization protests. In Miami, the city commission used the legal system to pass what probably was an unconstitutional law less than a week before the protest, giving the police authority to stop and search people who might be in violation. It was then rescinded before any legal challenges were issued. The fact that nobody was charged with violating the ordinance points to a strategy: a law can be temporarily applied to specific instances and then discarded. By the time that law is challenged in the courts, it is no longer needed for the specific protest it was designed to regulate.

In Miami, the Streets and Sidewalks Ordinance temporarily expanded the authority of the police so that they could (and did) conduct searches and seizures of anti-globalization activists with the excuse of looking for outlawed materials. Because any hard object was outlawed, police had broad latitude. It is telling, however, that out of the two hundred individuals arrested in Miami, not one was charged with violating the Streets and Sidewalks Ordinance. When arresting activists, police fell back on traditional charges, such as blocking a thoroughfare or disobeying an officer of the law. The ordinance's control strategy had less to do with actually arresting activists than with expanding the powers of surveillance and intimidation. By criminalizing everyday objects such as bottles and batteries, the city widened the net of possible violations.

Reviving Old Laws

Instead of creating temporary ordinances, some cities revive old, generally forgotten laws that are already on the books and then applied them specifically to the anti-globalization movement. Before the World Economic Forum (WEF) protest in New York City, the New York Police Department called for a "zero tolerance" attitude toward "violent protesters." A reporter wrote that "Police Commissioner Raymond Kelly had quickly thrown down the gauntlet by declaring that anyone who broke jaywalking or other laws would be arrested without warning, and for good measure invoked an 1845 edict against wearing masks in public" (Mikulan 2002, 28). The 1845 law forbade three or more people to assemble in a public space while wearing masks. According to a New York police officer, the law dates back to a time when the city was targeting Ku Klux Klan members who were gathering in New York City.

Like Miami's Streets and Sidewalks Ordinance, the revival and invocation of the anti-mask law directly targeted the radical circles of the anti-globalization movement by criminalizing their specific protest tactics. Chuck, an activist and organizer with the Pagan Cluster, explains the situation well:

> There is a whole group of people [in the anti-globalization movement] who believe that wearing a mask is an act of solidarity and resistance on behalf of communities that can't show their faces. These could be people either in that particular community who can't show their faces out of fear of police retaliation, or international communities, such as the Zapatistas who fear for their lives. In some cases, people can't show their face because the police will target them for months or even years after the protest. And with masks we are not talking about black bandanas or ski masks, but festive masks. So the police are making festive masks illegal, mainly to mess with the movement. They also understand the ideological conflicts within the movement, and they try to pit folk against each other.

As Chuck notes, wearing masks can be an act of solidarity, a way to challenge centralized authority and protest surveillance and intimidation. Masks have other uses as well. They offer a theatrical, festive expression of dissent that challenges the common perception that protesters are angry people. For example, in New York City I participated in street theater with a group called Art and Revolution. Its purpose was to bring people together to "create new ways to effectively resist and to build communities of resistance capable of making radical change and social revolution" (Art and Revolution 2004). Working alongside activists from several nations, we performed first at a public park located at Fifth Avenue and Central Park.

The piece included several scenes, about seventy individuals, several costume changes, and multiple sets of puppets (some representing "the community," others meant to be "the capitalists"). Individuals operating the community puppets (symbolizing earth and sustainability) entered first. Then the capitalist puppets

4-2. Protesters built this puppet during the 2003 WTO protest in Cancun. It represents the Mayan god Chac. (Photograph by Luis Fernandez and Sue Hilderbrand)

entered, dressed in ponchos with black top hats, holding huge wineglasses that looked like Earth. Drunk on gasoline and power, the capitalists pushed aside the community puppets. In the course of the story, activists dressed in seed, corn, and other plant costumes (and some wore masks) symbolically stomped on the capitalist class. In the end, everyone broke into a giant dance while drum rhythms washed over the crowd. The performance ran for about thirty minutes and was repeated several times along the four-mile march through New York City.

Because many of us were fully costumed and wearing masks, both during the performance and the march, we were breaking the law and risked arrest because we had covered our faces in public spaces. Yet no one in our theater group was arrested. Instead, several anarchists, wearing black bandanas over their faces, were singled out and removed from the march, even though they had not done anything different from what we had done.

Law enforcement's selective application of the anti-mask law had an interesting effect on protesters. Importantly, public announcement of the law months before the protest helped build an atmosphere of fear. In turn, this fear created conflict in the movement, as I witnessed in New York. At a spokescouncil meeting held late at night in a community church, about three hundred activists gathered to plan activities for the following day. About an hour into the meeting, the discussion turned to the issue of masks. A young female activist wanted to know if people would wear them or not. An older male activist, perhaps a veteran of many protests, expressed reservations regarding masks, saying, "I'd rather not be standing next to you when you put on a mask because the cops are going to attack you and me, and I am not looking for that." Others expressed similar fears about being targeted by police during the legal march. Yet some contested the idea that wearing a mask should constitute breaking the law. After a heated debate, activists agreed that they would bring masks but would wear them only if the police attacked first. There was considerable tension throughout the meeting, enough to threaten the solidarity of the group.

The law's effect, then, was not so much in its implementation but in its effect on activists before and during the protest. Like the Streets and Sidewalks Ordinance, the anti-mask law had less to do with direct repression and more to do with a softer mode of control, regardless of the law's original intended purpose. The threat of the law works from the inside out, forcing compliance in the movement through fear rather than through direct hard-line repression. We will see this situation many times as we explore the subtler forms of control.

Regulating Protest

During my interviews with activists, several individuals reported experiencing harassment that involved the use of city, county, and state zoning regulations. To understand this mode of control and its effects on the movement, we must first briefly look at how the movement organizes before each protest. Initially, organizations put out national and international calls for action six months to a year before a protest. For example, six months before the WTO protest in Cancun, a group known as Equipo Rumbo a Cancun (Team Bound for Cancun) put out an international call inviting activists from the "many headed hydra of resistance [to celebrate] the possibility of another world that we hold in our hearts and are building together, today":

> From the vast nuclei of organization, in Cancun itself, in Mexico City, in Chiapas, in California, in Seattle, and on the East Coast, we have a growing number of groups and committees self-organizing on the road to Cancun. In Mexico, farmers groups and trade unions are assembling in caravans. Political parties and grass roots organisations are mobilizing their rank and file, from Zapatistas to Electricistas,

women's groups to student groups, the sea of protest gath-
ers. Internationally, farmers in Central America, the landless
in Brazil, fishermen and women in India, environmentalists
from the U.S., and organic producers of Europe have
booked their tickets. Globally, activists from thousands of
NGO's, unions, affinity groups and independent media are
preparing to descend upon Cancun for another unforget-
table week in September.

In 5 months time we have the opportunity to confront
the WTO and effectively stop its itinerary, its crusading
agenda to open up economies (Laissez-Faire), to strike
down national laws that "hinder" free trade, and give the
nod to punitive sanctions on countries that fail to adhere to
its free trade gospel. In 5 months we have the opportunity
to gather once more, united in voice and purpose to
demonstrate the strength and vitality of our movement of
movements. In 5 months we will answer the urgent need to
act in this time of capitalist accumulation and resource wars
to say ¡YaBasta!, and demonstrate that another world is not
only possible, but growing here right now, with us, in our
struggle, in our action and in our practice (Equipo Rumbo
a Cancun 2004).

Activists put out similar calls to action for the protests in
New York, Miami, Washington, and Calgary. These calls mark
the beginning of protest planning. In most cases, local organizers
from the region lead the planning. If a region has few or no local
organizers in the area, then some activists will move to the location several months before the event.[2] These movement scouts
play an important role. They meet with local organizations,
apply for permits (if local groups need or want them), find housing for protestors yet to arrive, and secure meeting spaces. The
scouts live for months in a foreign city, getting the movement
ready to receive thousands of people during the days of action.

As a form of social control, zoning ordinances significantly affect these scouting activists. Many of the people I interviewed mentioned them as a form of harassment. Sandy, for instance, is an activist who arrives early to organize at many protests. "There are ways that zoning ordinances are used against the movement before the protest even starts," she reports. "We are there trying to get the resources we need with very limited cash. So the spaces that we secure [for meetings and sleeping] are not in the best parts of town. And our spaces become vulnerable to fire codes, building codes, insurance issues, or even food handling problems."

Zoning laws were influential in the 2000 IMF/WB protests in Washington, D.C. Attempting to strike a blow at the center of the anti-globalization movement, the Metropolitan Police Department of the District of Columbia, with the help of the city fire chief, raided the convergence center, which served as protest headquarters in the days before the protest. Using the pretext of a fire-code violation, the police entered the building and confiscated all puppets, banners, and medical supplies stored there. Sandy described the event:

> In D.C. the police raided the convergence space and shut it down for good. Their rationale was some kind of fire-code violation. They said we had bomb-making materials and chemical weapons. That amounted to paint brushes and rags in jars and chili peppers in the kitchen. They also got us for illegal cooking, or something like that. What happened was that we were using a propane stove to make our food. It turns out to be illegal to cook indoors with this stove, but the kicker was that the stove was not really inside but in an open-air garage. They still used that to enter the building and shut it down, making it much more difficult for us to build puppets and banners.

By this action, the police did more than confiscate materials: they successfully disrupted the ability of demonstrators to organize and conduct nonviolent training sessions. In the end, the police dismissed all charges against those arrested at the convergence center. But as one activist noted, the damage to the movement was done, regardless of the final legal outcome.

According to my interviews with activists, police also use building-code violations to harass activists. Chuck described a situation he faced at the FTAA protest: "In Miami there was a city inspection of the building where we were staying. They said there were some violations with the number of people we had in the building and some other stuff. However, we had lawyers with us. So we were able to fight them off. But that is the kind of stuff they do to activists if they can get away with it."

The police also draw on public health ordinances to target activists, specifically those dealing with the distribution of free food. A primary target is Food Not Bombs (FNB), which is composed of hundreds of autonomous chapters with members who prepare and share free vegetarian food with hungry people and protesters. The group has chapters throughout the world, including the Americas, Europe, Asia, and Australia (Butler and McHenry 2000) and is a staple at anti-globalization protests.

During the IMF protest in Washington, D.C., a fellow protestor and I had been running around for several days helping to organize communication for several marches. On the last day of actions, we were exhausted, having had only several hours of sleep in two days. At one point, we sought shelter at a local park and attempted to nap on a park bench. Unfortunately, we were awakened by a police officer, who used a bullhorn to inform us that we could not legally sleep in the park. Almost sleepwalking, we wandered out of the park and found some friends, who told us that FNB had set up a stand nearby where we could eat, drink, and rest. FNB provides such shelters not only for tired protesters but also for homeless people and other marginalized communities. Nevertheless, these public food and rest areas are illegal because they violate several public health codes, meaning that FNB activists are open to police harassment.[3]

NEGOTIATING DISSENT:
THE PERMIT PROCESS

As a form of control, law enforcement uses permits to "negotiate" the time, location, duration, and route of marches as well as the creation of protest zones, which define spaces for dissent. Law enforcement also constrains activists who are looking for temporary housing and meeting spaces in the host city. As I noted in Chapter 1, academic work amply documents the emergence of the protest permit process in the United States. In their discussion of the negotiated model of policing, Clark McPhail and colleagues (1998) provide a lengthy analysis of that process, showing that the U.S. Supreme Court, through a series of cases from the 1960s to the 1990s, compiled a substantial body of legal decisions protecting protesters' First Amendment rights. Known as the public forum laws, these decisions rely on the distinction between public and private space. Although they allow the regulation of public forums, the laws apply only to the how, when, and where of protest, not to the content of what protesters can say.

To preserve neutrality, public forum laws can only place "reasonable" restrictions on time, place, and manner. Nevertheless, they have set the stage for the bureaucratic regulation of protest. According to McPhail and colleagues, permits are central to the negotiated management model of policing protest because police are less likely to use force and therefore repress movements. Yet these authors do not discuss the full negative impact of such soft-line control tactics on dissent. In my view, permits are as detrimental to social movements as hard-line repressive tactics are. Their control is subtle, requiring protesters' consent and self-regulation for success. They shape behavior through internalization and consent rather than coercion, an approach that works well with a multitude such as the anti-globalization movement.

All of the police officers I interviewed described permits as central to their protest planning process. "The prevention [of violence] starts prior to a protest with the permit process," said a lieutenant with Washington, D.C.'s, police department. First, months before a protest, police can predict the number of officers necessary to patrol the event. According to a public information officer with the Miami Police Department, the permit process is useful for "getting an estimate on the number and type of organizations that might be attending the protest. Based on meetings and permit requests we get a good idea of what type of crowd to expect, and how to prepare for them." The permit process, then, brings police and protesters face to face before the event and allows police to collect data on the movement.

Second, police use permits to gain the upper hand in their dealings with protesters. An operations commander for the New York City Police Department described how police view the permit process: "A lot of times [protesters] will apply to demonstrate in certain areas, and we will deny that. For example, if people want to march down Broadway in the middle of a workday, we would deny that because it would inconvenience a lot of [non-protesters]." This sounds like a reasonable cause for denial or restriction and supports the arguments of the negotiated management model. Yet the process of denial and approval can be manipulated according to police preferences rather than practical considerations. For example, at several protests I attended, the permit process required marches to end at locations that were strategically beneficial to police but detrimental to activists. During the WEF protest in New York, for instance, the police issued a permit for a march that ended four city blocks away from the Waldorf-Astoria Hotel, where WEF members were gathering. The police prepared for the large crowds that they knew would end up in that location and successfully cordoned them off. This placed the protesters far from the forum delegates, out of view of the media, and isolated in a location that police could easily control. There was a similar situation in Washington, D.C., during the IMF/WB protests: at the end of a permitted march, police assembled thousands of officers who successfully contained marchers several blocks away from where the meetings were taking place.

Third, police are able to collect information on groups expected to attend the protest. Because the permit process requires organizers to name the lead organization, the police can identify cooperative groups along with their leaders, thus reinforcing (or creating) a distinction between "good" and "bad" protesters. Those who negotiate with police through the permit process are "good" protesters. Those who do not are "bad." Scholars have found that police tend to be more tolerant of "good" protesters (Jimenez and Reinares 1998; Waddington 1998, 1999; Noakes and Sieminski 2001).

This split between "good" and "bad" protesters creates tensions at planning and spokescouncil meetings and makes coordination and solidarity among organizers more difficult. For example, during the IMF/WB protest in 2002, I witnessed two separate organizing groups, each with a distinct convergence center and spokescouncil. One was called the Mobilization for Global Justice (MGJ), one the Anti-Capitalist Convergence (ACC). MGJ's leadership was more likely to negotiate with police, while ACC had anarchist members who were averse to speaking with police before or during a protest. As a result, the week's events were disjointed. There were two primary actions. ACC's included unpermitted demonstrations and disruptive tactics, all organized under the banner of "The People's Strike." MGJ's action was a permitted march ending at WB headquarters. In effect, police negotiations undermined solidarity in the movement, creating twice the work and half as many people in the streets.

Fourth, police use the permit process to educate protesters on what is and is not allowed, setting the tone and boundaries of protest before it starts. A Washington, D.C., police lieutenant explained: "We have certain requirements for permit applications for people that want to protest in streets and public spaces. During the process of applying for the permit we will, of course, sit down with the protesters and let them know what is acceptable and what is not acceptable. . . . We explain what is illegal and not illegal and ask them not be involved in the illegal conduct. It is a form of setting a boundary, but it is not that demanding." This officer, who is central to the planning for major protests in the Washington, D.C., area, sees the permit process as reasonable. A Miami officer expressed a similar sentiment:

> We use permits to educate the public and organization leaders. We need to educate them on what the laws are here, the laws for peaceful assembly or ordinances. The leaders of these groups are aware of what they want to accomplish throughout the event. But they need to understand and respect what we need. So we tell them what our expectations are. For example, we had a question regarding the size of the poles that needed to be used for signage and different items that were not allowed in the City. In every city there are ordinances that exist. And sometimes people are not aware of those ordinances because they vary from city to city, county to county, and state to state. So we educate them on what the city policies are, what the laws are.

Although police believe that permits are ways to communicate boundaries, negotiating about permits can pose several problems for protesters. Sandy explained:

> If you are looking for a straight-up legally permitted event, rally, march or whatever, then you have to get a permit. Once you decide to get a permit, however, you enter into a process of negotiation. Once you start the process, the police are going to start asking you all these questions that you may or may not want to answer. And they are going to want to get agreements out of you that you may or may not

be able to uphold. And if you can't, then they paint you as the person responsible for breaking the agreements. And they understand that. It is a set-up. . . . Once you enter this process there is a certain level of control that you give up over the event. When you speak with police, you have to make all sorts of concessions, like the route, the starting time, location, etc. And if you negotiate with police you also start having problems with your credibility and good faith with certain parts of the movement.

While negotiating with the police makes some parts of a protest less difficult for activists (such as securing a safe location and a march route), it also gives police information about the types of activities that will take place, the groups attending, and the number of people expected at the protest. Thus, it helps police maintain order, a goal that seems reasonable. Yet a primary aspect of a powerful protest is its ability to disrupt. If you remove this power, then the protest is less effective and perhaps less successful.

As Sandy pointed out, the permit process also places an unreasonable burden on those doing the negotiating. Police want agreements from negotiators regarding situations over which they have little control. For example, the New York City police educated protesters about the anti-mask rule. Yet negotiators could not control each individual's behavior, and the situation created internal conflict in the movement that led to a split.

Chuck described other limitations to negotiation: "[The police] will often give you a permit but stipulate that you can't march in this direction, at this time, or that you can't have puppets, or you have to end in such and such location. They will define what you can or can't have in your demonstration. They may say no to music or to vehicles, for no apparent reason. Through the use of permits they get to define the characteristics

of the game they want to play. So police definitely control
through permits, and maybe even [intentionally] create conflict
within the movement."

According to some activists, having a permit does not guarantee protesters the rights stipulated in the agreement. In
Miami, for instance, the AFL-CIO negotiated a permitted
march with the city police. During that march, police revoked
the permit, turning what started as a legal protest into a mass act
of civil disobedience, mostly unbeknownst to those taking part.

CLOSING PUBLIC SPACE

The closing of public spaces to activists is a growing tactic in
policing dissent. Like other examples, it does not rely on hard-
line repression but works softly and subtly, even making the state
appear generous and protective of protesters. In the end, however, such practices make mobilization more difficult and costly.

One of the first tasks of anti-globalization organizers is to
find places for protesters to meet and sleep. As I have mentioned, activists begin looking for free space months before a
protest. These places may include schools, churches, parks, or
other public areas. Without such spaces, there is no place to
organize, no spokescouncil, and no convergence center.

Early in the process, police enter into what Chuck calls a
"housing game":

> They always play the housing game with us. We start by ask-
> ing them to give us sleeping space. The city has three
> choices: they deny us housing, they provide housing, or
> they don't say anything about housing. If activists are not
> organized, then they will not say anything. If activists push
> hard, then they may say maybe. Or they will say no. Or they
> will say yes at first and then will withdraw the offer and say
> no. Or they will hold that no until about a week before the
> action. The point is that they make a housing crisis, hoping

that people will not come, hoping that people will be nervous about not knowing where they are going to sleep. Then during the final week, they will usually give us a location but not always an activist-friendly location. And it always has stipulations, such as you can only use the space between these hours or you have to be in and out by these dates, time that sometimes do not match the protests.

Housing was a particular issue at the G8 protest in Calgary because the town was too small to house thousands of protesters. To highlight the lack of sleeping space (and perhaps to dissuade protesters from coming), Canadian Prime Minister Jean Chrétien taunted protesters by saying, "If you want to come [to Calgary], bring a sleeping bag" (Pertuiset and Lemieux 2002). Activists took Chrétien's comments to heart and began to organize. To solve the sleeping problem, they planned to build a solidarity village that would house 10,000 protesters. They wanted to create a festival of resistance with big-name musicians, workshops, and a meeting space, a place where activists could also receive medical assistance and legal aid if needed. Unfortunately, the Canadian government officially closed all public lands near the G8 meeting location. Those lands were open only to "those officially welcomed by Ottawa" (Pertuiset and Lemieux 2002).

Organizers turned to private land as an alternative. They tried to lease land from the Stoney First Nation, a native tribal group with land close to Calgary. On the verge of signing a deal, activists learned that the Canadian government's security service had given the Stoney 300,000 U.S. dollars for the rights to the land (Rubinstein 2002). Protesters were left scrambling to find another location. Reportedly, the government was using the land for police "capacity building," including first aid and CPR training. In reality, the government probably paid to prevent anti-globalization protesters from being housed so close to the meetings.

In a final move to keep the solidarity village idea alive, organizers turned to the city of Calgary, some fifty miles away from Kananaskis Village, the location of the G8 meetings. Protest organizers asked the city to open public parks and buildings to house the coming protesters. The city council promptly denied the request, declaring that "no political gatherings are allowed in city parks" (Rubinstein 2002). In the end, organizers were unable to build a solidarity village. Although it is difficult to estimate the impact that these actions had on the activist turnout in Calgary, I personally know several individuals who did not participate in the protest because there seemed to be no housing space available.

Police and city officials used similar tactics in Miami before the FTAA protest. Looking to secure sleeping and meeting spaces, organizers asked officials to open public parks, churches, and city buildings. They started by writing an official document and submitting it directly to the city. "At first, the city looked like they were going to give us indoor housing, with restrooms and all," says David, an activist organizer. "But after they agreed to the housing, they quickly pulled out. Instead, they came back and said they would provide us [with] an empty lot, and they would put in toilets and water." In the end, the empty lot was an inconvenient and unsafe location for activists to gather. It went mostly unused during the protests, while activists scrambled to find other meeting and sleeping locations.

At one point, activists secured a local church as a possible organizing space. David described what happened next: "[After we secured the space] the police came over a few days later and told church officials that they could not house activists because it was illegal. If they disobeyed, they would be fined by the city. The church, of course, had to pull out."

DURING THE PROTEST

Legal control during a protest plays a lesser role than it does before or after a protest. David explained, "One of the things that we all know in the movement is that once the protest starts, once we hit the streets, the law doesn't mean a thing. The police can do anything they want, arrest us for things we didn't do. The arrests never stick in court, but that don't mean a thing. In the streets they can do anything." I heard this sentiment during several interviews with protest organizers and personally experienced the phenomenon at several protests. The rights protected by the First Amendment—freedom of expression and freedom of assembly—sometimes disappear in the middle of a contentious action. As Chuck said, "What is or is not legal behavior by the police during a protest is only worked out in court after the protest." While police told me that they always followed the law and protected the right of individuals to assemble, movement organizers had different experiences.

It is common for local police departments to assemble policing manuals that list all possible charges that officers can use to arrest protesters, which are distributed to the officers who are working at the event. The actual arresting charge varies from protest to protest, due in part to city and state code variations. John, an officer with the Royal Canadian Mounted Police, described how police officers use the law during a protest:

> There are all sorts of laws we can use. There are laws that will prevent people from walking on the street, for example. If it became necessary, you might use some of those municipal laws or state laws to prevent things from getting out of hand. Then you have all your criminal laws, like mischief, trespassing, property destruction, and all those. If things go as planned, and people are being cooperative, and they are dissatisfied with things, about expressing them legally, then common sense prevails. When things start to go a little bit wrong, then the contacts that have been made [through negotiations] with protestors can be used to inform protesters. Then it is up to them whether they get arrested or not.

Laws that police use during a protest vary from jaywalking violations to vandalism, trespassing, disobeying a lawful order, and failure to disperse. The document "Crowd Management and Civil Disobedience Guidelines" (California Commission on Peace Officer Standards and Training 2003) lists approximately 150 possible code violations that police officers can use to arrest protesters. They include general penal and vehicle codes as well as more obscure election and weapons laws. During an interview, a lieutenant with the Washington, D.C., police described his preference:

> There is one [law] that we use that I like very much. It's entitled incommoding, which is three or more people blocking free pedestrian traffic. There are other traffic laws that we use quite extensively, like failing to obey a traffic officer. But this requires several warnings, having to tell people that they have to get out of the street or they will get arrested. Eventually, if we need to, we end up making arrests for that type of conduct.
>
> We have certain ordinances about bonfires that we use as well. The statute is very old; however, it prevents open fire in the street. We use this one to arrest people that might be burning flags. Burning a flag in effigy is not a crime, but the fire needed to burn the flag is. So we arrest them on that. Fire tends to be a way to attract people and get them involved in more atrocious conduct. But the Supreme Court said that you could not get arrested for burning a flag. The charge now is kindling a fire.

The field of legal control encompasses the use of city ordinances, zoning restrictions, the negotiation of dissent, and the closing of public spaces. Together, these tactics place a burden on activists and easily meet the definition of repression (that is, any act that raises the cost of collective action). Although such tactics are less noticeable than traditional observations of police repression, they cumulatively restrain the actions available to protesters, rendering them less disruptive. In turn, this makes them less likely to produce social change. While mostly invisible to the media, social movement scholars, and the public, these soft forms of legal control, if left unchecked, will continue to harm activists while significantly restricting dissent.

CHAPTER 5

This Is What Democracy Looks Like?

THE PHYSICAL CONTROL OF SPACE

IN 1999, THE WORLD TRADE ORGANIZATION met in Seattle to launch a millennial round of trade negotiations. Along with the meeting attendees came thousands of protesters from all over the world who engaged in large street demonstrations outside the meeting venues. Using a network-based model, protesters organized around affinity groups to block traffic, close intersections, and lock down entrances to buildings. Catching the police and the WTO mostly by surprise, the protesters successfully shut down the city for several days. The demonstrations were so disruptive that the WTO had to postpone its trade negotiation until a subsequent meeting two years later.

Shortly after the Battle of Seattle, the Rand Corporation (funded by the U.S. Department of Defense) analyzed the success of the anti-globalization movement and the failings of Seattle law enforcement. The analysis described all the players and their strategies and examined why the movement had succeeded so well at disrupting the ministerial meetings (Armond 2001). The report concluded that law enforcement agencies were ill prepared to deal with this new defused form of organizing.

Since then, law enforcement has developed several tactics to deal with these challenges. Aiming to control a decentralized mode of organizing, police have begun to secure space, erect barricades, create security (or frozen) zones, and engage in mass preemptive arrests. This refinement in tactics is the state's response to an emerging multitude-like mobilization. Instead of relying on negotiations and permits to engage protesters, it has moved to control the physical landscape around a protest, aiming to prevent another Battle of Seattle.

Physical control of space refers to ways in which police departments carefully select and map out the material environment before and during a protest. By definition, a protest movement requires a contentious, prolonged challenge against powerful opponents (Tarrow 1998). To keep pressure on opponents, mass movements turn to public demonstrations aimed at publicizing their grievances and winning over public opinion. By necessity, this entails the assemblage of large numbers of people in the streets or other public areas (Mitchell 2003). As Don Mitchell argues, public space is intricately tied to social struggle because movements make their grievances known in public space. Contentious politics become visible in the streets, where protesters challenge authority.

Selecting Defensible Locations

The control of space starts with the selection of the geographical location for the summit or ministerial meeting. Shortly after the WTO protest in Seattle, globacracies, along with law enforcement, learned a key lesson: meeting location is an important aspect of dealing with potential protester disruption. Seattle was a poor choice for a WTO meeting because it was the hub for several radical movements. Today ministerial institutions carefully select difficult-to-access locations for their meetings, which makes mass mobilization more difficult. Rather than choosing cities or regions with vibrant social movements (such as Seattle or other cities in the Pacific Northwest), globacracies now choose locations that are easily defensible by the police and military, not readily accessible to protesters, and have little or no local movement history. For example, two years after the Seattle debacle, the WTO met in Qatar. Located on a peninsula bordering the Persian Gulf and Saudi Arabia, Qatar is a Muslim state ruled by a monarchy dating back to the mid-1800s (U.S. Central Intelligence Agency 2004). Qatar's government does not allow political demonstrations and severely limits freedom of association. In addition, due to strict immigration laws, it is almost impossible for protest organizers to enter Qatar to do the groundwork necessary to launch a successful protest. Thus, the WTO, with the help of the Qatar government, stopped all protest at its 2001 ministerial meeting. Yet selecting such an authoritarian state as a location lent support to the argument that the WTO was itself an authoritarian institution that did not care about human rights.

The selection of Cancun, Mexico, for the 2003 WTO meeting followed a similar pattern. In addition to being a vacation resort, Cancun is also a strategic location for discouraging protest. Its physical environment is easily defensible. Geographically, Cancun is a narrow strip of land sixteen miles long and about one and a half miles wide, connected at each end to the mainland. Security for the meeting included heavily fortified checkpoints at each of the two entrances, with national police asking for identification cards and searching all vehicles going in and out of the area.

There is little, if any, history of political organizing in Cancun, which made mobilization difficult and unorganized. When protesters arrived there in the weeks before the protests, they found very few local contacts willing to help with the basic requirements for organization. In the end, activists were forced to stay in a small town nine miles from the ministerial meeting, mainly due to the prohibitive cost of the hotel area.

The G8 used a slightly different version of this tactic for their 2002 summit meetings. John, an officer with the National Security Investigative Service within the Royal Canadian

Mounted Police, described the selection process: "At first, it was expected that the G8 meeting would be held in Ottawa. When it became apparent that [the 2001 G8 meeting in] Genoa was a violent situation, the venue was moved from Ottawa to a more isolated geographical location in the Rockies, in the beautiful area of Alberta. This was done primarily for security reasons since this was a much more defensible location."

The resort was located in Kananaskis Village. According to media reports, "a security area with a radius of 6½ kilometers, about 4 miles, [was] established around Kananaskis Village. Camping and recreational facilities within this area [were] closed to the public . . . and north–south travel along Alberta Highway 40 [was] sharply restricted. In addition, a no-fly zone [was] established with a radius of 80 nautical miles around Kananaskis" ("Public Announcement" 2002). Protesters never got within viewing distance of the meeting. Instead, they had to settle for protesting in Calgary, some fifty miles from Kananaskis Village. As in Cancun, these protesters were geographically removed from the meeting location.

That tactic was repeated in June 2004 at the G8 summit in Georgia. Leaders of the eight most developed nations gathered at a resort on Sea Island, located sixty miles south of Savannah. The location was selected for its seclusion, which allowed for very tight security. No protesters were permitted on the island, and even journalists were restricted to Savannah.

The Planning Process

The next step in the physical control project is the planning process. Police departments, along with various other governmental agencies, undertake months of preparation before any march, action, or arrest happens on the streets. Since the Battle of Seattle and subsequent anti-globalization protests, police agencies who provide security take the threat of disruption seriously, coordinating between different law enforcement and service agencies and training officers about how to respond to the protest.

In a case study of the 1997 protest against the Asian Pacific Economic Cooperation summit held in Vancouver, Richard Ericson and Aaron Doyle (1999) found evidence of cooperation between Canadian and international policing agencies. Since then, such cooperation has been common, as I found in the anti-globalization protests I studied. From police interviews, I discovered that planning for protests starts with the coordination of various city, country, state, national, and international organizations. A commanding officer with the Domestic Security Branch of Special Operations for the Washington, D.C., police described the agencies relevant to his city:

> Every city agency has a part in it, whether it's the Department of Public Works for removal of things that could be used as projectiles, through the Department of Transportation to help us with the control of traffic in the outskirts of one of these things; through the fire department who may provide for medical services for protestors and police officers; all the way up to include the federal government, the FBI and all sorts of intelligence networks. . . .
>
> We also take information from police agencies where they have large globalization protests. For example, we spoke with police officers in Genoa. We spoke with police officers from France, Canada, Scandinavia, Mexico. Anywhere we can gather information on who might be headed our way.

Officers from other policing agencies reported a similar process. Speaking about the planning for the 2002 G8 protest in Calgary, John explained:

> We start months before the protest by establishing partnerships with local police in various jurisdictions. So when you start [the planning process], you automatically include the

local police, who, in most cases, is the municipal police. We also include our provincial policing partners, which in the case of the U.S. would be the state police. So, we start by covering all aspects of the policing departments, including municipal, state, and federal level. In our case the federal police is the RCMP [Royal Canadian Mounted Police].

In addition, we draw upon the intelligence agencies, which in the case of Canada is CSIS [the Canadian Security Intelligence Service]. CSIS is equivalent to the CIA. We, RCMP, are like the FBI. We also work with our department of national defense because they have an intelligence component and immigration personnel. But the core group is always your law enforcement and intelligence components. In this capacity we worked as a team. The RCMP is usually responsible for coordinating things. But I always approach it is as a team effort, you know, the sharing of information among the groups that make up the joint intelligence group.

In all of the cases I studied, the planning process started at least seven months before the protest, when police gathered relevant policing and service agencies to coordinate a response. The local police department usually headed the effort, with other agencies providing support. For the 2003 FTAA protest in Miami, the police department acted as the primary leader in coordinating police response to the protest. The planning team included "25 local law enforcement agencies, 7 state agencies and 7 federal agencies" (City of Miami Police Department 2004, 1). Approximately forty law enforcement agencies participated in policing the Miami protest. Coordinating this massive response required a strict, military-style organizational structure with a single agency in command. The police department later described the team's structure and organizational style as "perhaps . . . without precedent in American law enforcement" (1). Miami's response had a more centralized command structure than did police response to other protests, perhaps because the city was the first to have the U.S. Department of Homeland Security as a major partner; and its success in subduing protesters may signal a trend in how police will plan for future protests.

There is also a trend toward using municipal and city organizations to help control protests. As discussed in Chapter 4, police use city codes, zoning laws, and fire violations to regulate the system. Use of these techniques is usually facilitated through local fire departments and city agencies that work as part of the coordinating team. In other words, the coordinating team functions as a resource center; and police agencies can share information and request assistance from any of the participating organizations.

The period before a protest also includes intense police training. All the officers I interviewed reported that police training was an important aspect of their planning process. As an extreme example, officers from Miami trained for six months before the protest. This level of training was "unprecedented in scope, intensity and the number of agencies involved" (City of Miami Police Department 2004, 4).

To meet its goal of training local and collaborating enforcement agencies on "the latest techniques in civil disorder management," the city used contractors from the U.S. Department of Homeland Security's Office of Domestic Preparedness (4). In addition, instructors from the New York City Police Department; the Washington, D.C., Metropolitan Police Department; the Arizona Department of Public Safety, the Santa Monica City Attorney's Office; the Morris County Prosecutor's Office; and the County of Los Angeles Fire Department trained local commanders on various protest policing techniques. Over six months, local commanders were instructed in "History of Riotous Behavior and Lessons Learned, Planning, Training and Intelligence, Community and Media Relations, Demonstrator

Tactics, Riot Control Agents and Less Lethal Munitions, Incident Command Systems, Legal Perspectives, Fire Ground Tactics, Doctrinal Concepts, Team Tactics, Force Multipliers, and Multi-Casualty/Mass Decontamination Scenes" (5).

The department also provided training for lieutenants and sergeants from various local police departments on "demonstration team tactics," teaching groups of officers how to maneuver around crowds. Training included "protestor extraction techniques" used by "extraction teams"—plainclothes officers who arrest "violent individuals committing attacks from within the cover of the crowds" (6). Officers from the Miami Police Department, along with their law enforcement partners, received additional training on legal issues, bicycle response tactics, SWAT team support, mass arrest procedures, and media training.

Finally, all response teams playing a significant role during the FTAA protest took part in a simulation exercise conducted in the designated protest area in downtown Miami, which made the exercise more realistic for the training officers.

> The Response Teams were required to utilize all the formations that had been taught to them over the previous months. These formations included columns, skirmish lines, skirmish lines with close support, wedges, wedges with close support, moving the crowd by advancing the platoon at a half-step, and moving a crowd by advancing the platoon with a controlled rush. The Cut Teams used extraction tools to overcome actual "sleeping dragons" and other protestor devices. The Bayside Market was cleared of plainclothes officers posing as resistant and violent protestors. The Bayfront Amphitheater was similarly cleared and secured. The Bomb Squad rendered safe a mock explosive device. The Technical Support Detail cleared a street of dumped sand and removed hanging banners from traffic

signals. The plainclothes extraction team members effected arrests from a crowd while receiving tactical support from a Response Platoon. And the SWAT Team entered and secured a school bus (9).

As the involvement of paramilitary units such as SWAT teams demonstrates, this training reinforces military-like attitudes toward the policing of protest. Yet the use of military equipment, training, and enforcement is not new to policing. For instance, Peter Kraska (1997, 2001) documents a sharp rise in police military units and a rapid expansion in military-style activity among police departments throughout the United States. What is new is the intensity of the training and the level of preparation that law enforcement undertakes before a protest.

THE ECONOMY OF PROTEST

Since the Battle of Seattle, an economy has developed around training officers and cities hosting anti-globalization protests. Security for each protest costs the local government

5-1. Police line up in Miami to push back protestors during the 2003 FTAA protest. (Photograph © Bette Lee)

millions of dollars, placing a large burden on the city or region hosting the meeting. For example, during the 2002 WEF protest in New York City, police overtime alone cost approximately 11 million dollars; policing the 2002 IMF/WB protest cost roughly 14 million dollars; and the budget for the FTAA protest in Miami was 23.9 million dollars (Nesmith 2004). An estimated 24 million dollars were spent to secure the 2004 G8 meetings in Georgia, not including state-of-emergency funds.[1]

The high cost of hosting a meeting can create budget issues for local police. In the case of the IMF/WB protest, police funding played a central role in the planning process. Several months before the event, Washington, D.C., Police Chief Charles H. Ramsey expressed concern about the cost for local law enforcement agencies. Police officials warned that without federal assistance police "might be forced to patrol a smaller area, restrict delegates' movement or seek more help from federal law enforcement agencies or the National Guard" (Fahrenthold 2002, B1). According to the *Washington Post*, "some [police] jurisdictions have been reluctant to send officers to Washington because . . . the District might not be reimbursed for the cost of the extra police protection—and thus might not be able to pay officers from other departments" (B1). To solve the funding problem, President George W. Bush proposed that the federal government provide 15 million dollars for the 2003 fiscal year, earmarked to cover the costs of securing the meeting.

While much money is spent on police training, transportation, accommodations, and overtime pay, some funding also goes to contractors. For example, the Canadian government hired CPG International, one of the world's largest communication consulting firms, to develop and implement a security communication plan.

The War on Terrorism fuels and funds this developing security economy. Soon after the September 11, 2001, attacks in New York City and Washington, D.C., authorities in the

United States and elsewhere publicly equated anti-globalization activists with terrorists (Panitch 2002). They specifically targeted anarchists and other activists involved in direct action. To support the security efforts in Miami and "prevent terrorism," Congress gave Miami 8.5 million dollars specifically for the FTAA meetings. The funds came directly out of the 87 billion dollar measure passed by Congress to support the Iraq war (Blumner 2003).

INTELLIGENCE OPERATIONS

Intelligence gathering is a final component of police preparations. Police gather data by requiring permits, studying past protests, surveying open source information, and infiltrating the movement. Each of the officers I interviewed identified information gathering as a key component in planning for protests. An operations commander in the New York City Police Department explained the importance of intelligence in general: "When you know they're coming, the first thing you have to do is gain as much information about the protest and the movement as possible. How many people are you going to have? What are their plans? What groups are coming? Where are they going to march? Are violent protesters likely to be there? And then you figure out what kind of police and equipment you need to police the event."

As I discussed in Chapter 4, the permit process is one basic method of gathering intelligence. Social movement scholars have shown that public assembly permits, now required in most major U.S. cities, help police collect essential planning information (McCarthy and McPhail 1997, McPhail et al. 1998). Since the 1980s, police have used this method at most large protests, not just for the anti-globalization movement. Yet gathering intelligence on the anti-globalization movement has become more intense since the Seattle protests, when the police were relatively unaware of it (Armond 2001). Subsequent protests in

Quebec, Washington, D.C., and Genoa have built a base of information on tactics, groups, and actions. Therefore, studying past protests can be important preparation for police departments. For example, the Miami, Royal Canadian, and Washington, D.C., police gathered information from past protests to develop policing strategies for protests in their cities. A Miami communication officer described how his department started its planning process:

> There is a lot of planning that takes place before the protest, and most of it is research. We have to look at the event itself: where it has already taken place, what those experiences were like, and what the problems were. We learn from the experiences that all other law enforcement agencies have with these protests. Then you take the good and bad and bring it back home to implement. When we did our training, we focused specifically on situations that had happened at other FTAA meetings and at past protests. So we use all that information to train our officers. It required a lot of manpower hours for training and research, which was expensive. So we educated ourselves all about the groups that were coming to the city to protest. We obviously do our research, and we have intelligence about different groups that exist. Without getting very specific, we have information that we receive regarding these groups and their plans. So we obviously use that in our planning efforts.

A Canadian officer reported a similar planning pattern for G8 protest in 2003:

> Before a protest, there are security, logistics, and planning issues, not just for the event itself but also for the attendees. Then you have all the coordination of logistics involved when you have a large influx of police officers from various law enforcement agencies coming in to provide policing

during the event. From a policing perspective, we would like to get active as a group, as a sharing mechanism, early on. Usually with a major event like that we want to get running as soon as possible so we can get the intelligence process taken into high gear. So that is very crucial from a planning perspective so that all your partners can come on board, and you can develop a schedule for meetings, and a process for exchanging information, and a process for disseminating intelligence briefings to planners so that they are all aware of what might happen as early on as possible.

In Miami, intelligence gathering played a crucial role in policing the FTAA protest. According to the police department, intelligence was important because it allowed "law enforcement to receive advance warning and information on any preplanned attacks of the FTAA venue, police officers, private or public property or the security fence" (City of Miami Police Department 2004, 17). The department's "FTAA: After Action Review" describes how Miami police gathered intelligence in advance of the meeting:

> Intelligence officers visited other law enforcement agencies in cities to observe planned demonstrations involving the FTAA, the WTO or the World Bank. In cities such as Cancun, Washington D.C., Sacramento, and New York, the officers learned how the intelligence component functioned from their counterparts and by personally witnessing the handling of the events. They also obtained copies of after action reports and operational plans. It became clear from these out-of-town meetings that the two most important aspects of the intelligence component would be the development of sources of covert intelligence and the creation of undercover intelligence grids during the FTAA event. (18)

As Miami's "After Action Review" makes clear, police gather and use intelligence information from multiple sources—some overt, some covert. Collecting open source information is an overt approach. Open sources include statements that activists make in newspapers as well as plans or action calls posted on activist web pages. A Canadian intelligence officer summed up the process in his country:

> Quite often the individuals that tend to cause problems turn up in the papers and Internet sites. At no point do we want to prevent individuals from the right to lawful dissent and organizing and protesting. However, we have the same rights as in the U.S. to look at public information. We're not in the game of spying on individuals that are organizing. We are just looking for individuals who wish to cause acts of criminality during these events. We have all seen them: we saw them in Seattle; we saw them in Quebec City. Open source information, then, is one source of information. There are other sources of information that are available to us, but some of them, obviously, I can't discuss with you.

Likewise, a high-ranking officer in the Washington, D.C., Police Department said that he "looked at information on the Internet, newspapers, and other publications." He added, "We listen to the rhetoric that the groups [are] putting out prior to the protest. These people tend to be very vocal prior to an event." When asked about what kinds of information his department collected, the officer mentioned "the type of tactics used by demonstrators; whether they are violent or disruptive. We look at past tactics. Then we put things in place to try to prevent them from doing that."

When I asked officers about covert sources of information, they gave guarded answers. Several described using covert information from national and international intelligence agencies such as the Royal Canadian Mounted Police, the CIA, the FBI, and Interpol. John explained how the process works in Canada:

> Besides using our intelligence, we also reach out to our international partners. We usually do that through our liaison officers abroad. The RCMP has members working in a variety of countries around the world. And they have developed an effective network of contacts within the countries where they work. We use these contacts. Similarly, the FBI has officers working in Ottawa. We use these officers as points of contact, and use them particularly in the case of the G8. We call them and say we are interested in obtaining information on individuals that might be disruptive and are traveling. They will give us the information they have. We certainly do use police contacts and agencies from around the world. For the G8 in particular, there was a very close working relationship with many of the American agencies. Given the global situation of the time, it was imperative that we have this close tight working relationship with other agencies, which would include the FBI, Secret Service, and the usual mix.

While local or national police usually lead the planning process, officers or agents from various national law enforcement agencies are present before and during each protest. They perform primarily in a liaison capacity, due mainly to jurisdiction. John described the Canadian approach:

> When we were working in Italy [for the 2001 Genoa protest], there was a group of police officers from around the world as direct points of contact to the Italian police authorities. For example, they can come to us and say, "There are a couple of Canadians that were arrested by our police agency. Could you help us and provide background information or do some indices checks on these individuals?" We will provide that information through our contacts

back in Canada. Or we can provide information on who is traveling that could be a problem. They do the same for us here when we have a protest within our borders. It works very effectively.

Typically, the police assemble a joint intelligence team to facilitate the flow of overt and covert information within and among agencies. For example, the Miami police created an intelligence task force, which was responsible for "coordinating the intelligence components from the various law enforcement agencies while also serving as a clearing house for all the information gathered" (City of Miami Police Department 2004, 18).

Infiltration

When I asked directly about other covert sources of information, such as the infiltration of groups, all the officers declined to comment. Yet evidence suggests that police do infiltrate activist groups before and during a protest. That evidence comes from several sources, including interviews with activists, recently revealed information about the anti-war movement, statements from Miami's "After Action Review," and personal observation.

Several activists declared that they had experienced police infiltration in the movement. For example, Linda, a long-time activist and a member of the Rant Collective, said, "One of the things that they do now is that they are explicit about their infiltration into our movement. During the eighties, it was not explicit, although we knew it was happening. But now they are explicit. They are telling us, 'We are infiltrating you; we are doing surveillance on you; we are on your listservs.'" An activist named Rob expressed a similar sentiment: "Another way that [the police] try to intimidate us is by sending undercover police officers to infiltrate the movement. We know there are a lot of undercover police at our planning meetings and actions. Infiltration is very common."

These accounts are clearly hearsay. Yet it is reasonable to believe that, given the history of movement infiltration in the United States, undercover officers may frequent anti-globalization meetings and protests. Ward Churchill (2001), who has spent a lifetime documenting police infiltration of radical movements, notes that FBI surveillance and counterintelligence directed against radicals was standard procedure by the end of World War II. With the help of local police departments, the FBI also infiltrated many of the protest and radical groups of the 1960s and 1970s, including Students for a Democratic Society and the Black Panther Party. But these infiltrators went beyond collecting information on tactics: they set out to exacerbate ideological differences among and within groups, hoping to break groups apart and discourage cross-group coalitions.

In the 1970s, after the release of the COINTELPRO papers, Congress launched an investigation of the FBI, which revealed that the agency, along with foreign intelligence agencies, had spied on more than 10,000 U.S. citizens, including Martin Luther King, Jr.[2] To protect citizens from a serious misuse of power, Congress tried to pass restrictions limiting the ability of the FBI and other organizations to infiltrate and disrupt movements. Unfortunately, the proposed legislation failed to gain enough congressional support. Facing strong public outcry over the abuse of civil liberties, Attorney General Edward Levi established procedural guidelines in 1976 restricting how agencies could conduct internal security investigations (Chang 2002). In 1983, Attorney General William French Smith instituted more permissive guidelines. And on May 30, 2002, Attorney General John Ashcroft replaced those guidelines with an even more permissive set.

But none of these versions gave the state as much leeway and legitimacy as the USA PATRIOT Act did. These new guidelines, adopted after the terrorist attack on the World Trade Center and under the auspices of the War on Terrorism, presaged a return to a time when the FBI routinely watched organizations "without suspicion of criminal conduct, targeted groups for infiltration and disruption based on their ideology, and maintained dossiers on thousands of law-abiding citizens who had expressed political views of which the government disapproved" (Chang 2002, 37). Given this history, activists' perceptions of infiltration seem plausible.

On October 26, 2001, President Bush signed the USA PATRIOT Act into law.[3] The act enhanced the state's powers of infiltration and surveillance by expanding the definition and scope of terrorism to include domestic terrorism. Loosely defined by the act, *domestic terrorism* could apply to any domestic group involved in an act in which violence erupts (Chang 2002). The broadened definition allows the state to infiltrate and survey more groups and larger numbers of people then ever before.

Yet evidence suggests that infiltration and repression of the anti-globalization movement began before September 11, 2001 (della Porta and Tarrow 2001, Scher 2001, Steward 2001, Panitch 2002). Writing before the attacks, Abby Scher (2001) said, "Over the past year, the U.S. government has intensified its crackdown on political dissidents opposing corporate globalization . . . [and] undercover operatives are spying on protesters' planning meetings" (23). These coercive police tactics became even more prevalent after the terrorist attack in New York.

Recent conclusive evidence of infiltration comes from a case in Chicago involving organizations linked to the anti-war and anti-globalization movements. According to the *Chicago Sun Times*, in 2002 Chicago police officers infiltrated five protest groups who were "threatening to disrupt the Trans-Atlantic Business Dialogue—a meeting of international business leaders" (Main 2004, 26). The groups included the Chicago Direct Action Network, Anarchist Black Cross, the Autonomous Zone, the American Friends Service Committee, and Not in

Our Name. The first three groups are associated either with anarchist or direct action tactics; the last two are prominent anti-war groups.[4]

Fully aware of the history of infiltration and disruption of social movements in the United States, Not in Our Name (2004) issued a press release condemning police infiltration. In part, it read:

> We find it abhorrent that the government sent police spies into our meetings and events. We assume it was to photograph us, to tape record us, and to identify our leaders, among other things. Many of us remember similar operations during the Vietnam War and Black liberation movements that resulted in government frame-ups of righteous activists like Geronimo Pratt who spent over two decades of his life in a penitentiary. Some of the veterans from Chicago among us remember, only too well, how the police infiltrated the apartment of Fred Hampton, the leader of the Black Panther Party, and then helped to set him up to be murdered as he slept in 1969.

The Chicago police launched four more such infiltrations in 2003 but refused to identify which groups were under surveillance. Activists believe that increased infiltration into peace and social justice groups is in part encouraged by the FBI, who have "urged law enforcement agencies to step up intelligence gathering against the anti-war organizations" (Not in Our Name 2004). Since then, similar police infiltrations of such groups have occurred nationwide: in Fresno, California (Galvan 2004); Grand Rapids, Michigan ("Police Monitored Anti-War Rallies" 2004); and Albuquerque, New Mexico (Hovey 2003). There is reason to believe, then, that the USA PATRIOT Act, along with the fear of terrorism, has influenced an increase in infiltration.

Miami's "After Action Review" openly but vaguely describes police infiltration of the anti-globalization movement in the city before the FTAA protest: "Officers overtly monitored the groups by attending public meetings. They did not however host such meetings or bait individuals to conspire to commit crimes. All groups, but especially the radical groups, needed to be monitored through the Internet and other publicly-accessible media. In limited circumstances, certain radical groups and activities required monitoring by covert operations including the presence of undercover law enforcement officers and the debriefing of civilian informants" (City of Miami Police Department 2004, 18).

Although police in Miami and elsewhere deny disrupting movements and baiting "individuals to conspire to commit crimes," there is evidence to the contrary. Reporting on the FTAA Miami protest for an Internet magazine, Tom Hayden (2003), former leader of a 1960s anti-war group, described witnessing several undercover police agents start a skirmish with heavily armored Miami police officers: "The crowd predictably panicked, television cameras moved in, the police lines parted, and I watched through a nearby hotel window as two undercover officers disguised as 'anarchists,' thinking they were invisible, hugged each other. They excitedly pulled tasers and other weapons out of their camouflage cargo pants, and slipped away in an unmarked police van."

Hayden's observations suggest that, at least in Miami, police not only infiltrated the movement but also provoked violence, a tactic with a long history in the policing of social movements (Marx 1974, Churchill and Vander Wall 2002). Yet not all infiltration requires secrecy or disguise. An intelligence officer with the Royal Canadian Mounted Police described how his colleagues infiltrated the G8 protest in Calgary: "One thing we found useful was to have members in uniform infiltrate the crowd with video cameras. They were walking in the crowd videotaping some of the activities and the things that they were planning, which by itself provides us with information. We have eyes and ears all over the place."

Effects of Infiltration

Infiltration affects the movement in several ways. It allows police access to insider information about the movement, such as the location and routes of marches without permits and possible disruptive tactics (violent or nonviolent), and helps them identify and target leaders. Because a successful social movement requires innovation and surprise, police infiltrators do more than just prevent violence; they also minimize the success of any tactic, peaceful or otherwise.

With its nonhierarchical organizational structure and public approach to planning, the anti-globalization movement is particularly easy to infiltrate. To participate in a planning meeting, a person only has to do a simple web search, find the location of the meeting, and attend. While the affinity group model prevents infiltration, affinity groups still need to coordinate their efforts at open meetings; and infiltration of these meetings is not complicated.

The knowledge that police are gathering intelligence through infiltration frightens activists; and if left unchecked, this fear can lead to conflict and disruption at planning meetings. James, an experienced activist in the anti-globalization movement, explains the impact of infiltration:

> In the movement, there is a lot of fear of infiltration because of the history of infiltration. We know that we are infiltrated, but we don't know by whom or when. . . . Police have used this before, and it has been a successful tactic, such as in the sixties with COINTELPRO. With that fear, two things happen. One, we imprison ourselves. Two, we police ourselves. This is security culture, right? Quiet, don't talk about what we are planning. Security culture is effective sometimes, but in mass actions it is mostly ineffective. When you are trying to get a lot of people together to do something but you can't tell them what it is, then it will not

work. It is nonsense. So a first step toward controlling the movement is to induce fear in the movement. A second step is having people incite conflict. I have been at meetings where we are all on the same side but we are all arguing. Infiltration? Who knows! But we do know infiltration and disruption [are some] of the tools used in the past: infiltrate and incite fights internally. But fear is the big point because once we feel it we start to police ourselves. And when we police or imprison ourselves, we lose. So that happens all the time, and it is no accident.

For the police, then, inducing fear in activists is equally as useful as the information gathered through infiltration. Mass actions must be done in open forums, and fear of infiltration leads activists to adopt security measures that make organizing mass actions more difficult.

In response to this fear of infiltration, radical members of the movement have called for a security culture approach. Usually reserved for groups that are planning direct action, security culture means keeping information secure from infiltrators, thus rendering an action safer. To accomplish this, activists encourage groups to adopt attitudes that make security violations socially and morally unacceptable. Violations might include not talking about illegal activities, not discussing your own or somebody else's involvement plans for future action, not asking questions about direct actions when you are not directly connected, or not spreading rumors that somebody is an infiltrator ("Secure Culture Basics" 2003). Activists have suggested a number of sensible ways to deal with police infiltration. For instance, they warn against using real names in listservs when discussing plans for direct action and to be careful about what protesters post on web pages. In hopes of balancing infiltration concerns with the maintenance of solidarity, they warn others in the movement to be kind and respectful while teaching the culture of security.

Yet in my experience, security culture falls short of meeting these ideal expectations and causes a number of problems. In practice, its ideas become distorted. Rather than creating a secure place to organize, the culture heightens paranoia. While a certain degree of paranoia is sensible and healthy (particularly given the history of infiltration and disruption), too much is detrimental and can inhibit mobilization. According to Linda, police heighten paranoia as part of a campaign to disrupt. Infiltration "tends to instill fear in many young people in our movement. As a result, they fall back on security culture, which is a practice that, in the end, breeds distrust and paranoia. . . . It is a sophisticated campaign, and we keep falling in their trap by engaging in an organizing methodology that they know will do us in in the end." In other words, the threat of infiltration as much as actual infiltration causes internal disruption in the movement.

I experienced security culture and its related paranoia first-hand at the 2002 WEF protest in New York City. At the time, I was traveling with two friends: Rachel and Miguel. Rachel was an activist from my hometown; Miguel was an activist and reporter from Brazil, working for a radical magazine in that country and writing about the anti-globalization movement in North America. We planned to attend a spokescouncil meeting in hopes of joining the upcoming protest activities and were told about two possible meetings: one an all-anarchist meeting organized by a loose anarchist network called the Anti-Capitalist Convergence, the other a meeting of both anarchist and non-anarchist groups. We decided to attend the first spokescouncil. My field notes describe what happened next:

> After some moments of confusion, we figured out that the Anti-Capitalist Convergence meeting met back at the church in an hour. After fighting our way through the streets of New York, we finally arrived at the church. Standing outside was a young man seemingly keeping watch. I said hello.

He looked me up and down, trying to size me up. Looking directly, intensely at me, he said, "Come in." Inside the door there was a second young white male. This one was more confrontational. I said hi again. "Where you from?" he responded. "I am from Phoenix, from the Local to Global Collective." Studying us, he continued, "Did you drive out here?" I responded by laughing and saying, "No, that would take five days. We flew." He waited a moment, thinking. Then he said, "Welcome." I walked right in, seemingly passing whatever test that was. He did not ask Rachel a single question, either assuming she was with me or perhaps that she was not threatening. However, the guy stopped Miguel.

When asked who he was with, Miguel says, "I am a reporter with a radical Brazilian magazine." Hearing *reporter* but not *radical*, . . . the young man called some friends over and started an intense discussion with his friends. Miguel tried to explain again that he was with a radical magazine from Brazil; that he was not going to report on the meeting; that if he did write about it, it would be printed in a different country, weeks after the events. But the information was of little consequence.

We were told that in the last few weeks they had problems with reporters coming to the meetings and then reporting what they did in the paper the following morning, even identifying individuals. I was skeptical, thinking that they were paranoid.[5] After about fifteen minutes the young man agreed to let Miguel into the meeting, but only if he identified himself as a reporter when the meeting started. He could stay if [the other activists present] let him.

The meeting started with the facilitator asking if there were any journalists in the room. Miguel had to identify himself as a journalist, explaining his situation to the entire assembly. Let me repeat, there was a high level of paranoia here, with some people not wanting Miguel in the room at all. Others said, "Come on, we are all journalists since we can all write about this if we want." After a lengthy discussion they let Miguel stay. However, the feelings of paranoia continued. . . .

A young woman started the discussion by saying, "This is not a safe place. Don't say anything you don't want to share with the police. This is not a safe place." She interrupted a group of people who started to talk about several arrests they had witnessed early in the day, stating, "Remember this is not a safe place." Some reported that police were harassing activists that look like anarchists, pulling them out of crowds and talking to them. In some cases, we were told, they were arresting anarchists for no particular reason. People were paranoid and feeling like the police were targeting them, infiltrating their meetings, and disrupting from the inside.

After about a half hour, we walked out of the meeting, having never really felt welcomed. My friends and I had been interested in seeing how we might support this group. But fear of infiltration, supported by a security culture and general paranoia, pushed away potential allies and inhibited progress at the meeting. This, in the long run, is detrimental to the movement.

PATROLLING, HARASSING, DETAINING

About a week before a protest begins, a large number of activists arrive in town from various parts of the world. Coinciding with this increase, the police begin their first patrols, a preventive measure designed to send an early message to activists. According to Jake, an activist and organizer, the message is "we are here, and we are watching you." Jake described the patrols in greater detail:

Then when people start to arrive in town, you begin to see more and more police in the streets. They start to escalate contact. If there is a convergence space, then you see more patrols in that area. You see police cars parked outside activists' meeting places. You see vans taking pictures as you go in and out. . . . Then you have officers start to detain people and ask them questions, which is completely illegal. They profile people, ask them questions, search them with no legal reason for doing that. Again, they continue to build the campaign of fear. I have been followed a couple of different times where the police wanted to find out where we were going, so they will approach us and harass us.

Although none of the police officers I interviewed mentioned this patrol tactic, every single activist I talked to described it in detail. Emily, a young activist from California, said she felt harassed by police: "In Miami, we counted all the different types of police vehicles that drove by where we were staying. We saw obvious undercover police parked outside our hotel, . . . and we saw regular police cars as well as heavily armored ones. There was a huge array of vehicles going by every hour, obviously patrolling where we were staying." Linda described a similar experience: "Other things that police do to control us is that they run an intimidation campaign. They increase patrols, obvious forms of overt surveillance, and more than usual ticketing of minor offenses like jaywalking."

These intimidation tactics are intense and produce fear among activists. To maximize their effect, police commonly patrol the convergence center, where activists come to network and get information. I witnessed police patrolling this space at several protests. In Washington, D.C., I saw paddy wagons pull up and park in front of the convergence center—a particularly intimidating act, given that the police had raided the convergence center at a protest the year before. Throughout the week, I also saw marked police cars parked in the area so that officers could keep an eye on the center. In Cancun, I witnessed police

pickup trucks full of heavily armored officers circling the meeting space. In Miami, police harassed and stopped individuals
around the convergence center, at times citing them for traffic
violations or arresting them for minor incidents.

Amy, an activist with the Black Block, reported being followed and put under police surveillance:

> One day in Miami we were leafleting the neighborhood to
> let people know why we were protesting. We noticed that
> unmarked police cars were driving by where we were hand-
> ing out leaflets. We were being followed, which was odd to
> us because all we were doing was handing out leaflets. We
> got a little nervous and started to walk to another street.
> They started to follow us, so we split up and went in differ-
> ent directions. By the time we were done weaving in and
> out of places, we realized that we were being tailed by seven
> or eight cars, most of them unmarked. So we just gave up
> and went home. When we arrived at the place where we
> were staying, there was a squad car sitting outside our place.
> That is what I call harassment, trying to make people feel
> nervous by following them.

Also in Miami, Chris and five of his friends were arrested
for photographing police while the officers were questioning
people on the street. According to Chris, "the charge was
obstructing a street or highway. It was not what we were doing.
We were actually watching them harass some people who they
thought were protesters, but we could tell they were not. We
took a few pictures and they didn't like that. So they arrested us
for blocking the street." Chris was held in police custody for
eight hours, where he was questioned several times by "officers
from the police department, some feds, and some joint task
force." The police repeatedly asked him who he was, who he
was working with, and what he and his friends were doing.
After Chris refused to talk without a lawyer present, the officers

took twenty-seven pictures of him, issued him a traffic ticket, and released him on his own recognizance. Chris believes the police were building portfolios of protesters. Whether or not this is true, officers did detain and question these activists for eight hours for a minor traffic violation. Presumably, this is not standard police protocol for all traffic violators in Miami.

Reducing Anonymous Space

Reducing the anonymity of protesters who are demonstrating or marching in the streets is a central strategy in the policing of the anti-globalization movement. A Washington, D.C., police lieutenant who also teaches a course called "The Psychology of Mob Behavior" explained, "We try very much to prevent the feeling of anonymity. A person that feels anonymous in a march or protest is the person that is more likely to do a violent action and improper conduct." Police reduce anonymity by doing patrols, openly videotaping activists, and randomly detaining them. These tactics fix the disciplinary gaze on protesters, and police officers who plan for protest are well aware of the power of this gaze. As an approach, it dates back to at least the eighteenth century and the panopticon, a circular prison built around a central well from which prisoners were observed. Inmates in the prison internalized the guards' constant gaze and policed themselves, making control much easier. Foucault (1979) noted that the aim of this approach is to place the burden of discipline on the observed, thus interiorizing the power of observation to the point at which a watched person becomes his or her own observer and self-regulator.

Many aspects of contemporary society, from community policing tactics to national security investigations, have shifted toward reducing anonymity. Federal wire tapping is an obvious example, but the trend extends to everyday life. For instance, seemingly innocuous Neighborhood Watch programs require vigilant neighbors to monitor who lives on a block and reduce the anonymity of any outsider who enters the neighborhood. As a result, residents sometimes report innocent passersby to the police. Thus, use of this tactic against anti-globalization activists is typical of our pro-surveillance climate, and law enforcement's strategies are varied and often effective.

A commander with the New York City Police Department described his city's approach to reducing protesters' anonymity: "We have been doing this since the sixties here. We set up checkpoints around the perimeter so that people know they are being frisked and will not bring anything to the demonstration that could cause injury. It's all about letting them know we are watching them. Then they will behave themselves." A lieutenant from Washington, D.C., mentioned another tactic: "Cameras are one way to reduce anonymity. I am not telling all the different types of cameras we use, but we do use them." As I noted during a protest, his department sometimes places uniformed officers with camcorders in highly visible locations; I watched such officers videotaping the Black Block's every move.

But reducing anonymity does not necessarily require high-tech equipment. The lieutenant also described a more rudimentary method: "We put a police officer on top of a truck with a pen and paper, visible to the crowd. Those folks that see this officer are less likely to get involved in anything illegal if they know the police officer can identify them, hence the masks that the anarchists wear. [Our approach] is to prevent them from feeling anonymous, so they understand they are being watched." In Miami, police surrounded the FTAA meeting location with a steel fence. Behind the fence, the police placed several cherry pickers, which they used as elevated gun towers for armed police officers. The idea was simple: if the activists saw the armed officers, then they would be less likely to act out, violently or otherwise.

Aware of the tactic, activists in the movement take precautions against the police gaze while rebelling against it. An obvious

5-2. During the 2003 WTO protest in Cancun, Mexican university students wear masks in solidarity with those killed in the Zapatista uprising. (Photograph by Luis Fernandez and Sue Hilderbrand)

response is to wear gas masks, bandanas, scarves, and other face coverings. As a technique in activists' repertoire of contention, wearing masks during a protest serves several functions. One is to protect activists from tear gas, should police choose to use it. Another is to create a feeling of unity and solidarity among masked individuals. More abstractly, it is a rebellious act against state surveillance, a symbolic act of clandestinity. The Italian anti-globalization group Ya Basta!, for example, uses the concept of clandestinity to describe the state's power to erase the rights of individuals who enter a country without proper government documentation (Notes from Nowhere 2003). In solidarity with those undocumented immigrants, group members wear masks to declare their support for all individuals who must remain hidden. Meanwhile, police seek to minimize clandestinity as a mode of resistance—even, as I have discussed, by reviving laws that make masks illegal.

FORTIFYING SPACE

The space around WTO, G8, and IMF meetings strongly resembles a war zone, with armored vehicles and police in full riot gear, including dark padded uniforms, sturdy helmets, and large see-through shields, and wielding batons and other weaponry. Such militarization is particularly prominent around the actual buildings that house the global meeting. Although this fortification approach has rapidly become commonplace, it has not always been the norm. In the 1999 protest in Seattle, for example, protesters were able to shut down the WTO meetings by blocking key intersections as well as entrances to buildings that housed the delegates, primarily because there were no fences or other blockades in place. A Rand Corporation report entitled "Netwar in the Emerald City" discussed the failings of the Seattle police, arguing that "the central fact of the Seattle protests is the utter surprise and confusion during the initial confrontation" (Armond 2001, 202). According to the report, police were overwhelmed. First, there was no unified police command until well into the protest, making communication difficult across law enforcement agencies. Second, there were not enough on-duty police officers to secure the city. And third, the police were unprepared to deal with the movement's decentralized, nonhierarchical, and net-based organizational structure.

In later years, police developed tactics to minimize such actions at ministerial meetings. None of the protests I observed lacked a unified police command structure, perhaps because they all took place after Seattle and the World Trade Center attacks. Such command structures make it easier to coordinate policing efforts among multiple law enforcement agencies. In Miami, for instance, the command structure for the FTAA protest involved more than forty law enforcement agencies:

> In the initial planning phase, a single police Captain filled the roles of Incident Commander and Operations and

Planning Section Commander. The command structure continually expanded as required to meet the increasing demands. The final command configuration included the Miami Police Department's Deputy Chief as the Incident Commander, a Police Major as the Deputy Incident Commander, Police Commanders as the Commanders of Intelligence and the Hard Perimeter, and Captains in command of the Operations, Planning, and Finance Section with a lieutenant in charge of the Logistics Section. (City of Miami Police Department 2004, 10)

In addition, police departments have corrected the problem of too few officers on duty. During the first day of the Seattle protests, police assigned four hundred officers to the WTO demonstration (Armond 2001). In contrast, Miami had more than 3,000 officers (including some from other cities) working at the FTAA demonstration (Nesmith 2004). Police presence in the street was overwhelming. Similarly, during the WEF protest, some 5,000 undercover and uniformed New York City police officers secured key locations in Manhattan, including subway stations and Times Square. My field notes describe the environment in New York two days before the first protest:

After visiting the convergence center I took the subway to Times Square. When I got there, I was amazed to see the number of police officers. They were present in the subway station, at the entrance to the station, and all around the streets. There were hundreds of them. Some of them were just standing around chatting to each other. Others were clearly "protecting" what they consider to be anti-globalization targets. These included corporate franchises such as the Gap, Starbucks, and Citibank. . . .

The officers were large, burly men, some in plain clothes and others with more military-looking uniforms. Seeing so many officers left me feeling fearful, particularly since the press is equating protesters with terrorists here in New York. I counted ten white vans full of officers around the corner. And this is in Times Square, not the Waldorf-Astoria where the meetings are.

BUILDING FENCES

After the Seattle protest, police knew they had to devise ways to make it more difficult for protesters to shut down a meeting. A simple first solution was to fence off the building. According to Linda, "One strategy . . . is to erect a fence and get behind it to defend the space. They create a sort of fort, and they stand inside protecting the place." For the WEF protest in New York City, the police fortified the Waldorf-Astoria, raising fences around the hotel that made it impossible to get anywhere near the building. During the 2002 IMF/WB protest, police surrounded the World Bank headquarters with a fence. In order to see the WTO delegates in Cancun, activists would have had to scale or tear down two fences, hike nine miles to the conference center, and then face a second set of fences. Officers were placed every twenty to twenty-five feet along each set of fences. There were only two entrances to the convention center, both guarded by armed officers. It was basically impossible to enter the convention center without proper credentials.

Adapting to the fence tactics, activists have begun to use them as symbols of globalization, equating them to the national borders that keep people from moving freely across the globe. For example, during my trip to New York City, activists gave me a pamphlet that reproduced the words of the Subcomandante Marcos, a Zapatista leader in Mexico known for fighting for the rights of poor and indigenous people: "In any place in the world, anytime, any man or woman rebels to the point of tearing off the clothes that resignation has woven for them and cynicism has dyed gray. Any man or woman, of whatever color, in whatever tongue, speaks and says to himself, to herself: Enough

5-3. Police officers stand on a cherry picker behind a protective fence at the 2003 FTAA protest in Miami. (Photograph © Bette Lee)

is enough! *¡Ya Basta!* For struggling for a better world all of us are fenced in, threatened with death. The fence is reproduced globally."

Inspired by these words, some radical sections of the anti-globalization movement have targeted fences. Bringing them down has become a symbol of victory, a direct confrontation of globalization. Naomi, an activist with the Pagan Cluster, described the attitude against fences:

> Barricades are barricades, fences are fences, walls are walls. They are all usually meant to divide and conquer, to shield and separate. Whether it's the wall that separates the rich neighborhoods from the "other" . . . the wall that separates the Jews from the "other" . . . the fences that separate Government, Inc., from those who resist. . . . We are not cattle to be herded, prodded, poked, examined, corralled, or contained in any fence, no matter how pretty it looks.
>
> I believe the use of barricades is unconstitutional, immoral, and an affront against our freedom. The more they are used, the more conditioned the public and government officials are to their legitimacy. I believe any acceptance of barricades is a strategic mistake.

In Cancun, I watched activists tear down a fence constructed to keep them away from the convention center. Tearing down the fence, in this instance, was mostly a symbolic act; for its destruction still left protesters far from WTO meeting space. Yet as a Korean farmer put it, the act showed that no fence could hold the movement back.[6] My field notes describe what happened:

> The plan was to bring down the fence. . . . By the time I got to the fence, women were already holding hands about ten feet away from the fence. I walked between the wall and the women, but soon realized they wanted me out, and not just me but all men. They were creating a female space, a space where they could bring the wall down on their own. The men started to form a line about four feet behind the women, which I joined. The idea was brilliant! At the

previous march some men began to throw rocks at police, which troubled some of the women. A way to deal with these men was to create a women safe zone. So the space between the fence and us filled up with women. There were indigenous women, Italian, older, younger, you name it. Then backpacks full of bolt cutters appeared. Women surrounded them and handed them out to their sisters. They all started to cut the fence down, slowly but surely. They were attacking the fence, determined to bring it down. . . .

The activists from Korea had a difficult time understanding that this was supposed to be a woman's space. They wanted to bring the wall down, and they wanted to bring it down now. Eventually, the Koreans convinced everyone that they needed to use the ropes they had brought to bring down the wall. With the agreement of the crowd, the Koreans moved their rope to the front, tying it to the top of the fence. The process was slow and methodical. They would tie the rope, tell the crowd to pull; [the crowd] would, and part of the wall came down. They would tell the crowd to stop pulling, retie the rope on the fence in a more strategic spot, and then pull again. The process went on for another hour until a large area of the fence was gone. . . .

Then the most amazing thing occurred. Once the wall came down, leaving a gap large enough to drive a tank through, the Koreans asked the crowd to stop. This was a tense moment, with some folks wanting to confront the police head on, and [they were] dressed to do so. The Koreans, speaking through a megaphone and using translators, asked the crowd to sit. . . . The energy dissipated and the action ended, with no injuries.

Another way to fortify space is to create security, or frozen, zones. Without fences, police can secure entire areas of cities, keeping close watch on everyone who enters the area. The

FTAA protest in Miami is a clear example of this tactic. The entire area around the Intercontinental Hotel, where the delegates where staying, was divided into several security zones. Police built an inner and an outer perimeter around the hotel. The first perimeter was immediately around the hotel and involved the use of French barricades.[7] The second perimeter expanded considerably. In the third space the police created a soft perimeter that included almost the entire downtown area:

> After reviewing the conference locations and analyzing the potential threats based on past incidents and the promises of similar actions in Miami, the area immediately surrounding the host locales was broken down into Perimeters or Security Zones. . . .
>
> Construction of a fixed barrier system resulting in the sealing of the "Restricted Area" for the duration of the FTAA event commenced on Sunday afternoon, November 16th, with the removal of the barricades and the installation of the security fence. The security fence was rented at a total cost of nearly $200,000. It has a patented design that was created specifically to address unruly crowds seeking to breach security barriers. It is constructed of interlocking steel panels with tight mesh to prevent protestors from gaining a handgrip for either climbing or pulling on the fence. The fence has a metal plate attached at the bottom that extends approximately three feet towards the crowd. In order to get close enough to touch the fence, a protestor must stand on the attached metal plate. This plate prevents demonstrators from pushing over the fence, as they would be forced to also lift their own weight as they stand on the plate.
>
> With the installation of the security fence, the "Restricted Area" became a frozen zone with strict controls on access to the area until the end of the event. This Restricted Area had several access points, staffed on a 24-hour basis. All persons

wishing to gain access into the Restricted Area were required to have FTAA credentials. In the event a person did not have credentials, positive identification and verification that such a person was authorized entry into the Restricted Area was determined via the Command Post. Law enforcement officers were also required to present credentials to enter the Restricted Area.

The plan called for each hotel and business located within the restricted area to have designated access points to enter the area. Those designated access points were to be displayed on each individual's credentials. As discussed in the "Additional Issues" section of this report, the credential process was the responsibility of a non-law enforcement governmental agency. The original plan was determined to be faulty, however, enormous efforts by the law enforcement team resulted in the development of a contingency plan that limited the inconvenience caused by the initial breakdown in the credentialing process. . . .

A "soft perimeter" was also established with boundaries from NW/NE 6 Street on the north, Biscayne Boulevard on the east, NW/SW 2nd Avenue on the west, and the Miami River on the south. Although south of the Miami River, the Brickell Avenue Financial Corridor was also considered to be within the soft perimeter. The role of officers assigned to the soft perimeter was to monitor vehicle and pedestrian traffic entering the downtown area and maintain open the roadways along the perimeter. Staffing of the soft perimeter would not commence until 6 A.M. on Tuesday, November 18th. Vehicular and pedestrian traffic were free to travel within the soft perimeter, however an increased police presence was necessary due to the area's close proximity to FTAA locations, the existence of attractive or vulnerable targets and the need to keep traffic flowing through the busy downtown area. (City of Miami Police Department 2004, 11–12)

When protesters hit the streets of Miami, the police were ready for them. The space was divided, fortified, and policed. Law enforcement had the upper hand not only in weaponry and numbers but also in geography. And this tactic continues. When the G8 met in Germany in June 2007, German police erected a permanent seven-mile fence around the meeting location. Unlike previous fences, this one was bolted to the ground and reinforced with concrete.

CONTAINING THE RADICAL PLAGUE

Foucault's analogy of social control as disease control helps us understand how law enforcement treats and thinks about policing protest. Examining the power mechanisms involved, Foucault (1979) argued that control of the black plague in the fourteenth century required strict portioning of space as well as careful surveillance, inspection, and order so that the disease would not spread. This holds true for any plague, and policing radicals in the street takes a parallel approach.

One tactic is to contain, isolate, and separate activists so that the disturbance does not spread like a disease. Throughout history, police have developed various ways to control and contain a crowd, such as using lines of officers to push a group in a desired direction or officers on horses to clear a troublesome space. But groups in the anti-globalization movement are more difficult to police with these traditional methods. The decentralized, affinity group model, in which activists strike out in multiple locations at once, requires new methods. Today, in addition to building protected perimeters, police carefully divide the protest space into small sections for easy surveillance, as fourteenth-century officials did for plague control. In downtown Miami, for example, police used grids to keep tabs on the movement and minimize the possibility of surprise:

> Confidential surveillance grids were devised to keep tabs on developing threats during demonstrations and marches. The

intelligence component established a confidential number of permanent fixed grids around the downtown area and one roving grid. Officers in undercover roles were assigned to the grids. The leader of each grid was a Miami Police Officer or Sergeant.

The function of each grid officer was to monitor the area for any radical group activities and to file an immediate report to the Operations Center by phone or radio while still maintaining their undercover role. Officers were required to maintain grid integrity to limit the opportunity for a surprise attack occurring in one area while a diversionary action was taking place in another. As an additional set of eyes looking for spontaneous direct actions, the FBI and the Miami Police Department were jointly tasked with providing several electronic video-monitoring devices throughout the venue, which provided "live" video feed to the Operations Centers. (City of Miami Police Department 2004, 18)

In addition to responding to decentralized, affinity-based actions, police must contend with other protest tactics. Snake marches, for instance, are the movement's response to demonstration permits: rather than apply for a permit that requires police negotiation and a predetermined route, clusters of protesters wind in and out of streets. To deal with snake marches, police physically separate and isolate protesters from the larger public and each other. Sometimes a large number of officers in riot gear will surround the entire march, which may include twenty to five hundred people. At other times police will break the group into smaller units. Linda described the effects of this approach: "In Miami, there was a march that left from the convergence center of mostly Black Block folks. Soon after it left, the police came in and surrounded them all, completely surrounded them. Then they took them wherever they wanted them to go. The group I was with took off before they could get us. They wanted us to go to a certain route, and we just basically took off. But all they have to do is put up police lines in certain places to determine where we could and could not go. In the end, it felt like there was little we could do."

Police use a similar tactic on permitted marches that include small radical contingent. For example, the WEF protest march in New York City included about 10,000 marchers, among them members of the Black Block. The police used the permit process to establish a route for the march. Then they used barricades, officers, bikes, and motorcycles to restrict the march to a predetermined path, making it difficult for protesters to leave the group and nearly impossible for passersby to join. At one point, I observed what looked like the entire march contained between motorcycle officers on one side and a miles-long barricade on the other.

At the end of this march, the New York police used another common tactic, which I call corralling. It involves confining people into relatively small, fenced-off areas that police have established for control purposes. Knowing that protest march would end at the Waldorf-Astoria, police constructed a series of containment pens designed to hold 2,000 people each. When the marchers arrived, officers corralled them into these holding tanks. A city police lieutenant told me:

> We had a system of barricaded streets that we built. This is a system where we put people in pens, metal barricades. We make these large boxed-in areas where we know people are going to end up. We design breaks so that not everyone is in the same place. We try to make them substantial size, but small enough to break the groups down into manageable sections so that we can get into them in case people need help, if they are injured, or if they are doing something wrong. So we have access to them in the pen so that we can

do any type of police action. We do this systematic enough
so that we can control the crowd. We build one, fill it with
people, section it off, and then we build another, section it
off, and so on until the entire crowd is contained in neat
boxes.

The Washington, D.C., police used the same tactic during the
permitted march at the IFM/WB protest in 2002. A fortified
and barricaded space with hundreds of officers in riot gear
awaited the marchers at their destination.

PREEMPTIVE MASS ARRESTS AND SNATCH SQUADS

Along with containment and separation, police use targeted
and mass preemptive arrests to physically control the movement.
While there is scholarly work regarding the role of arrest to suppress dissent (Balbus 1973, Barkan 2001, Churchill and Vander
Wall 2002), most social movement scholars do not distinguish
between the types of arrests made but tend to treat all arrests
equally. My research suggests, however, that police make arrests
in three different ways: individually, *en masse*, and by snatch
squads.

Individual arrests are aimed at high-profile activists. Although
the movement is mostly nonhierarchical, certain people are
heavily involved in planning and coordinating protests. For purposes of this discussion, I call them *leaders*, but they would probably reject the term. In one case, John Sellers, an organizer with
the Ruckus Society, was arrested on the street while talking on
his phone outside the 2000 Republican National Convention in
Philadelphia. Police charged him with fourteen misdemeanors,
including jaywalking and using his cell phone to plan vandalism.
He was held in jail for the duration of the protest, with bail set
at 1 million dollars. When his case reached a judge, the prosecutor dropped all charges.

In the past, arresting movement leaders has effectively slowed the growth of movements (Barkan 2001). For instance, in the 1960s and 1970s, prominent leaders such as Martin Luther King, Jr., and Huey P. Newton were clear targets of the state. But in my experience, leader arrest is rare in the anti-globalization movement, primarily because leaders are difficult to identify. As an alternative, police have started using preemptive mass arrests to sweep the streets of troublesome activists—sometimes while they meet to organize, sometimes even when they peacefully gather in public areas.

In Philadelphia, just before the 2000 Republican National Convention, police surrounded and arrested seventy-five activists who were making large puppets for the upcoming demonstrations. With helicopters circling, officers rushed the building where, according to one of the activists present, "[we] were working, building and storing puppets for the political props." Amy, an activist in the movement, explained what she knows about the incident: "There was a raid at the puppet factory on A16, supposedly due to a fire-code violation. Then they claimed that they found weapons. But later it turned out that the weapons were just bottles of paint, and their charges did not stick." As in many protest-related arrests, all charges were eventually dropped.

While doing fieldwork, I narrowly escaped arrest in a similar incident in Washington, D.C. My field notes describe the event:

We walked slowly to Freedom Plaza, at Fourteenth Street and Penn, N.W. There was supposed to be a gathering there at 10 A.M. Organized by the Anti-Capitalist Convergence, the gathering is titled "Beat the Anti-War Drums: Percussion Protest—No War on Iraq." We were exhausted and were running about fifteen minutes late. By the time we arrived . . . the entire park was surrounded by police officers in full riot gear. There were police on motorcycles, on horses, and in vans; you name it. A helicopter noisily chopped around above our heads, providing an eerie, war-like atmosphere. It very much felt like the activists were against a mighty force.

As I got closer, I noticed that police officers (standing shoulder to shoulder) had encircled the entire park. Nobody could get in; nobody could get out. Inside the circle there were approximately five hundred people. Later I learned that police were waiting for the protesters to gather at the park. They knew the groups would gather here, brought in a large number of officers, and waited until the park hit critical mass before encircling everyone there, regardless of whether they were protesters or not. Arrested along with protesters were journalists and people that were just walking by on their way to work. I stood there for about an hour watching the police arrest all five hundred individuals, two at a time. They put them in ten large buses and charged them with failing to obey a police order.

Thus, in one sweep, the Washington, D.C., police removed five hundred radical activists from the protest, keeping them in jail over the weekend and away from the marches and protests planned for the coming days. When I asked officers from the city to speak about this incident, they declined to comment because of a pending legal case. A year after the event, all charges against those arrested at Freedom Plaza were dismissed due to improper police procedure: the police did not properly warn the crowd to disband (Leonnig 2003). Yet even though these arrests were illegal from the start, police are likely to reuse the tactic in the future.

Mass preemptive arrests may control radical activists, but the strategy is messy and sometimes leads to the arrest of passersby. To solve this problem, the police sometimes choose a more targeted approach. Snatch squads (as activists call them), or extraction teams (as police call them), are teams of officers who arrest activists during a moving march. The Miami police used this tactic at the FTAA protest:

> Plainclothes "extraction teams" were created for assignment inside the demonstrations or marches. For the most part, these plainclothes officers were to assume only an observation role. However, these officers were trained when to take police action, which included situations where a radical group member was causing significant property damage, committing a felonious act, or attacking innocent people. The undercover officer was instructed to ask for backup officers to assist him prior to engaging any radical group members.
>
> The extraction teams were intended to separate violent actors from within crowds without escalating a larger confrontation between the crowd and police. This dangerous assignment required swift action by the plainclothes officers in the face of expected attacks by those seeking to free their compatriots. The extraction team commander, a Miami Police Lieutenant, assembled a group of officers that marched alongside the radical groups during the FTAA event and provided valuable information on the plans and the mood of various individuals and groups. However, their effectiveness as arrest and extraction teams was hampered by the fact that their undercover roles were often detected by group members and the officers were greatly outnumbered by the more radical of the protest participants. (City of Miami Police Department 2004, 18–19)

In essence, snatch squads are specialty teams trained to infiltrate a march, observe activists, and arrest individuals intent on causing harm. Theoretically, they take a surgical approach to the task, removing specific activists or groups while leaving the rest of the march untouched. As far as activists are concerned, however, the practical application of snatch squads is far from ideal. Linda described her experience with snatch squads at several protests: "Snatch squads are these roving teams of police. They can be either dressed in uniform or undercover. But they are smaller, mobile groups of police that can move quickly and can go after people, break up situations, and snatch people from the middle of crowds. This was one of the most disconcerting strategies used in Miami. They were targeting specific people and also randomly arresting folks. They were undercover, embedded in the march, grabbing people and throwing them into vehicles and carrying them away. They were also grabbing people and pulling them behind police lines.

The physical control of space is central in the social control of dissent and the policing of protest. After the 1999 WTO protests in Seattle, police developed and adopted techniques designed to deal with a decentralized, nonhierarchical, network-based movement. Such policing required thoughtful planning and careful attention to the geographical space in order to control mass movements. Law enforcement adopted specific maneuvers and tactics designed to manipulate the space before and during large mobilizations of the anti-globalization movement. Until now, social movement scholars have mostly overlooked these control techniques. Yet if we want to understand the spatial dimensions of control, we must look beyond notions of repression as it occurs during a protest and examine the various ways in which police manipulate space in all phases of protest and planning to ensure strategic advantages.

CHAPTER 6

"Here Come the Anarchists"

THE PSYCHOLOGICAL CONTROL OF SPACE

LAW ENFORCEMENT USES numerous psychological tactics to control protest, constructing the meaning of anti-globalization activism through public relations campaigns and media messages. Psychological tactics are social control techniques that operate at the level of the mind, with the goal of creating fear and making it difficult for protesters to successfully mobilize. These police marketing efforts frame the movement as violent, dangerous, and irresponsible, heightening the anxieties of local residents as well as activists.

Psychological tactics, then, involve the cultural production of meaning. They are inherently about the struggle over how the general public understands and reacts to protesters. These tactics generally take the form of carefully manicured media campaigns that influence opinions and thus make it difficult for protesters to successfully mobilize people.

THE FRAMING PROCESS

To understand the cultural production of meaning as it relates to protests, social movement scholars have introduced the concept of framing (Gamson et al. 1982, Snow and Benford 1988). This is the process by which activists turn vague ideas and grievances into coherent arguments that mobilize people

138

(Snow et al. 1986, Tarrow 1992, Noonan 1995, McAdam 1996, Zald 1996, Benford and Snow 2000). Framing starts with the idea that social movements are already implicated in the recon-struction of reality. Benford and Snow (2000) describe it as *meaning work*—an active and contentious process of producing meaning to challenge existing conditions. From this perspective, social movements do not grow independently from larger struc-tural conditions. Instead, activists carefully, strategically, and col-lectively craft meaning around their contentious actions. These *collective action frames* help movements identify problems, com-municate them to a larger public, and mobilize individuals to join them (Benford and Snow 2000).

Much of the academic work on framing revolves around how social movements construct meaning to mobilize individu-als (Ayres 2004). How do movements frame their grievances? How do they use frames to attract and mobilize individuals to their cause? While these are important questions, they are only indirectly related to the social control process. I am interested in looking at the other side of the issue: how does the state, through law enforcement agencies, frame protest to minimize participation in movements?

PUBLIC RELATIONS EXPERTS

The framing process of social movements tends to be col-lective and organic. It usually involves limited resources and is conducted by activists or organizations with little or no budgets. In contrast, the framing resources available to the police are more extensive and often include trained public relations officers. Months before a protest, police develop and implement sophis-ticated communication strategies that sometimes involve hiring corporate consulting firms to implement multi-targeted media messages.

The policing of the 2002 G8 summit in Kananaskis Village, Alberta, is a clear case of how law enforcement agencies can use state resources to implement a media and communication campaign that decreases mobilization. Months before the protest, the Royal Canadian Mounted Police, along with the Calgary Police Service, hired GPC International to design and implement a communication strategy. GPC International is a partner company of Fleishman Hillard, one of the largest public relations firms in the world. The Canadian police were motivated to work on public relations because they had received negative publicity during the policing of previous large anti-globalization protests. In 2001, the Royal Canadian Mounted Police had attacked protesters at an international economic meeting in Ottawa, an action that was harshly criticized in national Canadian newspapers. That same year, Italian police had killed an anti-globalization protester at the G8 summit meeting in Genoa, resulting in mass protests across Europe. Because both the G8 and Canadian law enforcement needed a legitimacy boost, the police adopted a negotiated approach in Calgary.

During a telephone interview, a high-ranking employee of GPC International described his role in planning for the G8 protests:

> My first role was to stay at the offices here at GPC and write the strategic communication plan. I needed to identify the audiences, identify the messages, and design a multilevel communication approach. So essentially my role was to draft a document that described the strategic direction for the integrated policing team.
>
> Then the second role was the communications council. At that point I joined the team and moved into a separate building. I worked with a joint team, with an inspector from the Calgary Police Service and a sergeant from the RCMP. We had interconnections right up the highest areas of the police command structure.

In a document produced months after the event, the company described its communication approach:

> Drawn from a freshly crafted "Philosophical Framework" outlining the highest vision of summit security operations, new methods of outreach and engagement would be explored, and previous communications challenges would be revisited with an aim of learning from past failures to create future successes. As such, a joint Royal Canadian Mounted Police and Calgary Police Service "Public Affairs Communications Team," or PACT, was created. The PACT mandate was to develop innovative two-way communications with key stakeholders including municipal, provincial and federal governments, local businesses, nation-wide protest movements, environmental activists, Kananaskis area and Calgary residents, partner Summit agencies, mutual-aid police officers, and all levels of media. Public support for the G8 security operation was critical in order to retain legitimacy, and to keep open lines of communication, in the event of a security incident or altercation. (Larsen 2003, 1)

With the help of GPC International, the PACT was responsible for planning, coordinating, and implementing a communications approach for the larger G8 summit security team: "creating a positive image for the CPS [Canadian Police Service] and RCMP; managing public fear around security process and democratic values; creating a positive image for the CPS and the RCMP; managing public fear around security process and democratic values; ensuring feedback from key audiences, and responding appropriately; ensuring comprehensive internal communications both within the security planning group and, on a larger level, with G8 intra-government organizations, and; restoring long-term public confidence toward policing of international conferences" (2).

The PACT's overarching strategy was to develop and launch a public relations campaign tailored to various specific audiences; and one aim was to "enhance the organization of the RCMP and CPS, and affiliated agencies, while minimizing apprehension through proper planning, education and dialogue" (1). Because affirming police legitimacy was a central concern, the PACT publicly embraced the notion of cooperation. Rather than assuming an adversarial attitude (as was the case in Miami and New York), the team tried to create a communication bridge between various activist subgroups and the Canadian police. A GPC employee explained the process:

> So the first thing was strategy. What we basically did was make a list of all the people who we needed to talk to. So who do we need to talk to, what do we need to say, and what is the best way of saying it?
>
> We started by looking back at the history of these types of protests. One of the key things that we did in developing our strategy was trying to present to our police clients the difference between what you might call the prevalent public mindset, the activist mindset, and the police mindset going into this protest. In the past we had a lot of "we" versus "them" mentality. We the police, them the protesters. We wanted to get in a little deeper into what the mindset of the protestors was and to develop techniques that we could use to communicate with them in a more productive way rather than setting up those oppositional statements right away.
>
> We also talked a lot about an outreach approach targeted at various different audiences so that you have slightly different messages to different people. However, we would all be coming from the same core information. So it is not like you are changing who you are but changing the points of relevance to those people you are speaking to.

The PACT developed a multifaceted public relations campaign that addressed various groups differently, slightly altering the message to fit each audience. According to the GPC employee I interviewed, "the overarching message was that we [the police] want to work with you [the community]." From this basic message arose several more specifically targeted communications.

To develop good relations with the business community, the team asked for input on security measures. PACT members visited local businesses and talked with the Chamber of Commerce about how the G8 summit might affect them. "Our message to them was that there would be certain community measures in place that might inconvenience them. Our message was that we would communicate with them in an open way about the things that may have an impact on how they run their business." In addition, the team communicated the "level of security threat, so that you can make up your own mind and take independent action. . . . [We] gave them a threat level and then allowed the business to take their own actions." In the end, "what you would see is some business boarding up their windows and locking their buildings. And other businesses were comfortable with the security risk as explained by the security services."

Another stakeholder was the First Nation people who lived in the Calgary area. To secure Kananaskis for the G8 leaders, the police and the military had to place people and equipment on First Nation land. "Our message to the aboriginal people had more of a humanitarian edge rather than a financial one, like with the business folks. We let them know that there was going to be activity in traditional native grounds. How can we best negotiate with you [for] the use of the land? If we need to set up security towers, communication antennas, and campsites, where can we best do that so that we respect the right of the aboriginal people?" As negotiators, the PACT sent law enforcement officers who were also tribe members, which, according to the GPC employee, "proved quite useful in the end."

Another important outreach group included the protesters themselves. Hoping to start a dialogue, the PACT identified and contacted groups who had been present or active at previous anti-globalization protests in Canada. Communication officers from the team met with university student groups, environmentalists, and leaders of nongovernmental agencies. David, an officer with the Royal Canadian Mounted Police, described the initial contact with protesters:

> We started with the nonviolent groups, mostly the groups from the universities. These groups are familiar with what we were doing, with the concepts that we were using. What happened was that over time the word started to leak out that these guys, us, were actually listening to them; we are different from other cops. We actually discuss things with them. This started to bring other groups to us, the yellow groups, the ones that were a little more aggressive. We actually ended up traveling across Canada in February of 2001, with the Department of Foreign Affairs who was hosting the summit. . . . So we went to Vancouver to these meetings in case people had questions regarding security. Again, it was a lot of "what do you want to see from this protest?" And their response was "we want to be close enough so that our leaders see our message." We had to tell them that from a security vantage point we could not do that.

The PACT worked with protesters to negotiate routes and protest locations and to understand the issues important to activists. An officer with the Canadian Police Service described the attitude of the police toward the protesters: "We said to them, if you want to do a march, we are willing to walk right along with you. Obviously don't smash any windows since that would be crossing the line. But do your thing. If you want to sit down, sit down. If you want to turn right, turn right. On the other hand, we will also be there to make sure that the march goes on without difficulty." Thus, as prescribed by the negotiated model of policing, the PACT put an emphasis on communicating the boundaries of acceptable and unacceptable behavior.

The final key stakeholder, and the largest and most important subgroup, was the general population. To reach this stakeholder, the team sent out national and international advisories and used local media, posting public service announcements on the radio and running ads in local newspapers. They provided phone numbers and addresses so that the public could get answers to all security questions. The message, according to a GPC employee, was "we are here to protect the public interest. If you need anything, come talk to us and we will talk to you honestly."

Police interviews and my review of documents detailing the communications design leave little doubt that the PACT was intent on improving communication between the police and the public in order to change both police behavior and public attitudes about the policing of protest. Adopting a negotiated management approach rather than an escalation model, the police offered movement leaders concessions in return for an agreement to self-police (McCarthy and McPhail 1997, McPhail et al. 1998). To maximize a positive public perception, the PACT chose "key gatekeepers and facilitators" to communicate their targeted message to each subgroup. These individuals were respected community members whom the police could contact for dialogue if necessary: university student leaders, heads of First Nations, nonprofit agency staff members, business leaders, and representatives from local and national government agencies.

Once the PACT had created this multileveled public relations structure, it set out to deliver a message. A GPC employee summed up that message:

> Our golden rule was not to mix our messages. The first phase was about getting different people to understand that security is important, that security is done on different levels. . . .

Second was explaining who is going to actually do the work, or introducing the officers. So we rolled out the police officers that were going to be present in Calgary. There was the RCMP and the Calgary police. Once you have those two phases in place, when you have people saying, "I understand that security is important. I understand the difference between security for protesters and security for terrorists, and I understand who is going to do what. I believe in these people."

Then the third and final phase was to actually roll out the security methodology, which to be honest with you was pretty aggressive stuff. We were flying fighter planes *en masse*. If anybody got anywhere near the meeting, they would have been shot down; same thing with anybody that tried to infiltrate the areas where the leaders were gathering. We made it very clear to everyone that we had soldiers with live weapons. But we could not have done this, having fighter jets flying over people's farms, soldiers in the forest, without first having discussed the need to do this and explaining to them that these people would be there and the reasons they would be there for.

Unlike the collective action frames described by social movement scholars, the process of meaning making in this case resembled a marketing campaign in which companies create a need for a product and then sell the product to consumers. It is important to remember that law enforcement's process of creating meaning differs a great deal from the way in which movements frame their grievances. The difference starts with the amount of resources available to police as well as with the sophistication of their approach. The PACT set out to identify various audiences, develop multilevel selling points, educate each audience on its specific needs for security, and then present that audience with the agencies that would provide security. While the motives of the GPC consultants who worked with the PACT were admirable (to improve communication and modify policing behavior), ultimately the approach was still about control: to minimize disruption, to reduce protest to passive and ritualized dissent.

The PACT approach also emphasizes activists' great disadvantage in the struggle for public opinion and sympathy. Their tools and resources are limited. They can openly discuss and disagree about how to frame their grievances. They can make puppets and signs and perform street theater to catch the public eye. But they do not have access to sophisticated message campaigns created by public relations firms and aimed at numerous target audiences.

COURTING THE MEDIA

For all the protests I studied, the police developed and implemented public relation campaigns in the months leading up to the event. Some campaigns were sophisticated and well funded; others were less so. In addition, during each protest, all law enforcement agencies had coordinated communication centers to facilitate the flow of formal information from the police to various local, national, and international media institutions. Police communication at the FTAA protest in Miami illustrates this tactic. Unlike the Canadians, the Miami police neither adopted a negotiated management approach nor hired a public relations consultant. Instead, they handled their public relations campaign in house. This is not unusual: many large police departments have their own public information departments, often staffed with several public relations officers trained to handle the media and the public.

To coordinate the communication efforts of approximately forty law enforcement agencies, the Miami Police Department created a joint information task force, which served as a liaison to the media and did outreach in various communities. The task force was responsible for making information easily accessible to local, national, and international reporters. Housed in a central location, public relations officers could swiftly disseminate information. One of those officers, Carol, described why the police needed such a communication center: "If everyone in the world had a question and then you get referred to someplace else, then you get frustrated; you alienate the media that way. When they called us, we had people from each organization present in Miami in our facility; we could ask them directly about the appropriate information. This way we were providing the most correct, up-to-date information. If somebody called wanting information about an arrest or something, all I had to do was reach out to that person, and the info was there. Then [I'd] turn to the reporter and give it to them directly, friendly-like.

While a centralized information center does not ensure that media outlets automatically report events from law enforcement's perspective, it does mean that some of the information passed along to reporters gets reported as fact, is not double-checked for accuracy, and is not attributed to the police as the source. For example, weeks before the FTAA protest, the *Atlanta Journal-Constitution* reported that "10,000 to 100,000 demonstrators are expected in Miami during next month's ministerial meetings" (Chapman 2003, A5). The U.S. General Accounting Office (2003) had published that attendance estimate eight months before the protest, although its report did not explain how the figure had been calculated. The Office of U.S. Trade Representatives, which had disseminated the estimate, was in charge of planning logistics for the FTAA and was working closely with local law enforcement and national security agencies. In the months leading up to the protest, the media picked up the 100,000 estimate (eventually dropping the lower end of the range) and reported that figure as factual, broadcasting the impression that Miami would be invaded by protesters. In the end, only 25,000 to 30,000 protesters attended the event, far short of the highly exaggerated estimate proffered by the Office of U.S. Trade Representatives.

Why would the Office project such a large number? Perhaps it was being cautious, projecting a worst-case scenario so that police organizers could prepare appropriately. Carol told me, "The numbers fluctuated a lot, from 50,000 to 100,000 to 30,000. But we originally expected well over 50,000 people to come to the event because we thought there would be local and national protesters descending on our town and we wanted to be prepared. And we knew there would be a lot of media. But it was too large of a prediction in the end." Another possibility is that the trade office needed to imagine a threat large enough to attract financing for security needs. Spark, an anti-globalization activist, said, "I think the figure was so high because the police wanted to justify how much they were going to spend on security. Saying that many people were coming makes you feel like you are being invaded. And an invasion requires an army of protection, and [the police] are that army." Whatever the case, the effect of overprojection was clear; it heightened public fear of the protesters, allowed law enforcement to justify the high cost of security, and made local residents more willing to cooperate with law enforcement under the auspices of security.

Police also court the media by establishing close working relationships with reporters. For example, adopting the U.S. military media model in Iraq, the department embedded reporters with police teams on the frontlines of the protest.[1] During the event, reporters patrolled with several different units, including the patrol response platoon, bicycle response platoons, cut teams, and marine patrols. Carol told me that approximately twenty-four reporters were embedded on each of the three days of the protest, but she did not clarify how many total days the police allowed reporters to patrol. Embedded news organizations included the Associated Press, NBC, Reuters, the *Miami Herald*, the *South Florida Sun-Sentinel*, CNN, Fox, and several television stations, in addition to numerous local news outlets (La Corte 2003).

Yet reporters did more than just patrol with police during the protests. Weeks in advance, they were invited to participate in police-run training session covering topics such as "anticipated crowd actions, personal protective gear, police formations, and the potential use of weapons including batons, chemical and less lethal tools." According to police reports, "the training centered on the safe positioning of media personnel within these police elements. The media participants were instructed on the dangers of placing themselves between violent protestors and the police line" (City of Miami Police Department 2004, 7). While such training sessions might seem innocuous at first glance, they encourage reporters to cross a dangerous line: to risk entering into a joint operation and adopting police perspectives and attitudes against protesters.

From the police perspective, embedding reporters is a smart strategy because from the start it allows police to build relationships with individual reporters and frame protesters as violent. As Janet Lopez, director of communications for the city of Miami, explained, "protestors cause injuries to police officers. . . . [O]ur police department is not the aggressor. . . . They are public servants, and we hope [embedded] reporters will show that" (Rodriguez 2003).

Embedded media in Miami served other control functions as well. They allowed police to discriminate between "legitimate" and "illegitimate" news outlets. As I have discussed, Indymedia activists, who are members of an Internet-based network of independent media centers (IMCs), produce and post articles, news stories, personal accounts, and edited videos on websites across the world. Their goal is to keep other activists and the general public informed about protest actions. In Miami, these movement reporters became illegitimate reporters and did not have the same rights as reporters who were embedded with the police. Annie, an Indymedia reporter, explained, "[The police] know what we are doing, and it makes them nervous.

They know that we have video recorders and that we are watching them; that we are organized; and that if they do something wrong, we will catch it. And they don't want us around." She said that in Miami the police targeted movement reporters and confiscated cameras. A coalition called Save Our Civil Liberties confirmed this testimony, reporting that the police had confiscated or broken four broadcast-quality cameras in Miami (Carlson 2003). Naomi Klein (2003), a well-known movement journalist and author of the anti-corporate book *No Logo*, reported the following incident: "Independent journalists who dared to do their jobs and film the police violence up close were actively targeted. 'She is not with us,' one officer told another as they grabbed Ana Nogueira, a correspondent with Pacifica Radio's Democracy Now! who was covering a peaceful protest outside the Miami-Dade county jail. When the police established that Nogueira was 'not with us' (i.e., neither an embedded reporter nor an undercover cop) she was hauled away and charged" (25).

Embedding media is a relatively new technique, and it is not yet clear whether the tactic was effective in Miami: police received ample negative press coverage during and after the FTAA protest. But it is important to note that law enforcement is involved in an ongoing process of learning to control the flow of information. From a social control perspective, embedding reporters is an example of the evolution of the control of dissent through media management. It shows that police value the importance of media reports and understand the growing influence of independent media coverage.

COURTING THE PUBLIC

Public opinion plays a central role in the policing of protest. How the public feels about a movement or a protest and its policing reflects favorably or unfavorably on police departments and their leaders. To court the public, law enforcement needs a multilevel public relations campaign aimed simultaneously at the protests, the local community, and national and international audiences. A high-ranking officer with the Washington, D.C., police explained: "We try to get all the information we can to the media so that people know how violent these groups are and the type of things they might do because, . . . of course, we need the public support to do what we do. Without it, we can't do our job." Officers from other departments expressed a similar need for public support.

Of immediate importance for law enforcement is managing public perception in businesses and neighborhoods near the ministerial or summit meeting. Since the WTO protest in Seattle, law enforcement has learned to keep local businesses and residents in mind while preparing for anti-globalization protests, hoping to maintain a good working relation during and after the event. As part of its public relations campaign, for instance, the Miami Police Department put together a slideshow describing the coming protests and protesters and presented it to various downtown groups and businesses.[2] The stated purpose of the slideshow was to provide the community with background information about the FTAA, a history of other demonstrations, and planned police operations in Miami.

Analysis of the presentation offers insight into social control through public relations. At first glance, the fifty-slide show looks like an average public service announcement. A closer look, however, reveals two relevant points. First, the presentation suggests that the Miami police were interested in not only educating the public but also endorsing a proposed FTAA head-quarters in the city. For example, when explaining what the organization represents, the police stated: "The FTAA will eliminate trade and investment barriers on virtually all goods and services traded by member countries, reducing prices for consumers and creating a new market for producers throughout the hemisphere" (City of Miami Police Department 2003, 4). The police explained that the city is competing to "become the permanent U.S. headquarters to the FTAA secretariat," which will bring with it "89,000 direct and indirect jobs," "add 13.5 billion annually to Florida's Gross State Product," and make the port of Miami "the largest port in the *World*" (8–9, emphasis in original). With such laudatory language, the police moved from a neutral institution tasked with protecting public safety to an organization working hand in hand with globacracies to promote their ideology.

Second, the slide presentation framed the movement as violent, thus instilling public fear of the protesters. Police accomplished this goal subtly, by way of a mixed message telling the community to be calm while warning them of coming violence. The "After Action Review" stresses how the city and the police tried to maintain a calm atmosphere:

> An enormous effort was undertaken by the Mayor of Miami, the Chief of Police and his leadership staff to ease the concerns and fears generated by the media portrayal of violence and destruction. Police officers and supervisors personally visited scores of businesses in downtown Miami. The Mayor, the Chief and the City's Community Relations Board took advantage of media interviews to spread a message of calm. The police leadership delivered the same message to all our law enforcement partners. The Chief generated a video message for all officers that sought to calm their anxieties and remind them of their obligation of professionalism and restraint. One week prior to the FTAA, the Chief also personally spoke to the Greater Miami Chamber of Commerce luncheon and urged the attendees to keep their companies open and continue their business as usual. The message was constant; while minor inconveniences

were possible, the police could guarantee their safety so they should not panic nor close their operations. (City of Miami Police Department 2004, 3)

During telephone interviews, officers to whom I spoke made similar claims. Yet those interviews also revealed a more complex message:

In the case of the FTAA, we wanted people to feel calm. However, there were groups, and we always emphasize that it was small groups, that identify themselves as Anarchist. And those particular groups were saying that they were going to be defiant to the laws of the City; they were going to come down and they were going to be violent. Now you have to be aware of that possible threat, but you have to be careful not to overshadow the event with that because in actuality you have a lot of larger groups that are peaceful and requested to come to Miami legally. These include union members and different type of peaceful organizations. But there is always the small group of violent protesters that can cause a lot of trouble, and we had to let the public know about them.

In other words, police asked the public to remain calm while telling them to brace for violence.

Although both the "After Action Review" and police officers themselves claimed that law enforcement tried to ease public fears, the slideshow suggests otherwise, stating that "peaceful groups are usually accompanied by a small (2%) but historically violent group who's [sic] intent is to disrupt the meetings" (City of Miami Police Department 2003, 16). Police described the tactics at past protests as ranging from passive resistance to "active resistance, non-compliance, [and] aggression toward public or police" (18). They warned that protesters would obstruct traffic, major thoroughfares, hotels, businesses, and other public venues.

The final protest tactic, according to the presentation, would be "anarchy" (24). Presumably, police were referring to a state of chaos rather than to anarchist theories of self-rule, autonomy, and mutual aid.[3]

Such mixed messages were repeated in the media. Speaking to a reporter, a Miami police lieutenant affirmed that 98 percent of those coming to Miami were peaceful protesters. "But that 2 percent is pretty troublesome. . . . [W]e have been preparing unlike anything we've ever prepared for in the Police Department" (Hirsh 2003, 1A). Adding to public fears, the *Capital Times* reported that police were protecting the FTAA members from the anarchists who "want to kill you" (Novak 2003, 14A).

A similar pattern occurred before other protests. For instance, one Washington, D.C., officer claimed, "We do not set the stage before the events by using the media. We provide service at a protest, and we will intervene when appropriate. We don't scare the public. We only give them the information that we have." Yet during the week leading up to the 2002 protests, law enforcement agencies issued press releases containing information that may indeed have scared the public. For example, Police Chief Charles Ramsey publicly stated that anti-globalization protesters could hinder the department's ability to respond to terrorist attacks (Taylor and Cella 2002). That same week, the FBI's cyber-crime division issued a public warning: "Some protestors may be planning criminal or violent activity—especially against local branches of companies or organizations that represent capitalism and globalization. In addition, a small group that intends to disrupt the meetings with a physical attack may use cyber means to enhance the effects of the physical attack or to complicate the response by emergency services to the attack. The cyber portion of this attack can be executed by sympathetic hackers or by mercenary hackers seeking publicity" (U.S. Department of Homeland Security 2002). The warning correctly stated that law enforcement had collected no evidence of a "direct threat against the IMF or World Bank." Nevertheless, it advised that hackers might still attack. These types of warnings play on deeply rooted societal fears of terrorism and disruption, which are then transferred to the anti-globalization movement.

Police emphatically deny setting the public against protesters. But consciously or not, their statements and warnings produce fear in the community. That fear works as a control mechanism, creating heightened awareness, anxiety, and a desire for police security. It also creates a hostile atmosphere for protesters, which can make mobilization of the local population difficult and reduce available resources. Protesters have little chance to convey their message to people who might join or be sympathetic to the movement. For instance, in Cancun, police referred to anti-globalization activists as violent, calling them *globophobes* (*globofobicos* in Spanish) who were fearful of an economically developed Mexico.[4] As a result, the local community became afraid of the protesters in their city.

THE VIOLENT ANARCHIST FRAME

Examination of the media coverage before an anti-globalization protest reveals a clear pattern of messages, and most salient is the violent anarchist frame by which both police and news outlets equate violence with anarchism. This frame is closely related to what Robert Benford and David Snow (2000) term *strategic process framing*, which is "deliberative, utilitarian, and goal directed" (624). In the cases I have studied, law enforcement and globacracy representatives use the violent anarchist frame to produce fear in the population, which facilitates a more cooperative public environment and induces a chilling effect on both the public and the activists.

Although the violent anarchist frame has a long history, it came to fore shortly after the 1999 WTO protests in Seattle, when Black Block anarchists (referred to in the media as the "Eugene Anarchists" because they supposedly came from Eugene, Oregon) broke windows at carefully selected corporate targets such as Nike and Starbucks. Images of the Black Block and the broken windows entered the public consciousness and were seen as primary tactics of the movement. Since them, "the anarchists are coming" message is often broadcast in the months before a protest, which has not only frightened the public but created internal splits in the movement; and fear of anarchists has only increased since September 11, 2001.

To fully comprehend the deep roots of the violence frame, we must examine the context of security in the post–9/11 world. The connection between the anti-globalization movement and terrorism is a classic case of what social movement scholars term *frame bridging*—linking two or more similar but socially unconnected frames that relate to a particular issue (della Porta and Diani 1999). Shortly after the terrorist attacks, local authorities (along with representatives from global institutions) publicly equated protest against globalization with terrorism (Panitch 2002). Since then, activists in the movement have interacted with a public that perceives them as violent and a possible national security threat.

Several scholars have noted that the violence frame poses a serious public perception dilemma for the anti-globalization movement (Epstein 2001, Buttel and Gould 2004). According to Frederik H. Buttel and Kenneth Gould, the *violence* label attracts much-needed media attention, allowing activists to make their grievances known to a larger public. Yet media coverage of acts such as breaking windows tends to be negative, which isolates radical sections from not only the public but also other groups in the movement.[5] Some of these views on the dilemmas of violence, however, miss an important point: media-reported violence is already implicated and intertwined with mechanisms of control that use the framing process to mitigate the movement's impact. That is, talking about violence as a dilemma fails to acknowledge that violence is now a trope attached to the movement. It no longer matters if the violence originates with police or with anarchists. The framework is already in place; and once something happens, the public interprets the violence as an anarchist act.

The violent anarchist frame generally begins to take shape at least three months before a meeting, when police publicly predict the arrival of thousands of protesters in their city, some of them violent anarchists. For example, three months before the 2002 G8 protests in Canada, a Calgary newspaper reported the following information:

> Canada's spy agency has quietly warned government officials of possible violence by fringe anarchists at the meeting of G8 leaders in Alberta this June.
>
> A newly obtained report, prepared by the Canadian Security Intelligence Service, says radical Black Block elements that disrupted previous international summits likely will organize for the conference for the leading industrialized nations in the resort village of Kananaskis.
>
> The intelligence report, distributed last December to key federal agencies, argues that some anti-globalization groups are calling for "a diversity of tactics, which in the past has been seen as a tacit approval of violent assaults against the police. . . . The anti-globalization movement will continue to regroup and pursue its various goals. The vast majority of protesters will attempt to stage non-violent demonstrations. Those who support the use of violence, including anarchists, will continue to do so. . . . Given the fringe anarchist element involved in these protests, the possibility of violence during the G8 meeting cannot be ruled out." (Bronskill 2002b, A3)

A month later, an Ottawa paper ran a follow-up story warning the public that "militants aim to take the capital":

> Beneath the stark and buzzing fluorescent lights of L'X, a dilapidated concert hall on Montreal's east side, a group of

50 militant radicals planned and plotted for "physical confrontation" in Ottawa next month. . . .

They spoke of snake marches and blockades along roads leading into Ottawa in the days ahead of the June 26–27 G8 summit in Kananaskis, Alberta.

They spoke of using a "diversity of tactics"—including possible "violence"—to deliver their message. They earmarked corporate and political targets. They spoke of "solidarity" and the "armed tactics" of their comrades in uprisings as far away as Mexico. . . .

The 35 radical protest groups planning to make the trip to Ottawa from as far away as New York and London, Ont., use a range of tactics, from public education campaigns to forms of violent direct action. (Mills 2002, B1)

The newspaper treated the word *violence* loosely and mostly quoted it out of context. As commonly connoted, violence conjures up images of individuals who are injuring or killing other people. But the reporter did not distinguish between property damage and damage to human beings, an important difference for movement activists. Such news coverage was common in the days before the protest, hinting at possible anarchist attacks on the public when in reality that threat was minimal or nonexistent.

Two weeks before the G8 protest, the *Ottawa Citizen* again reported that anarchists were a large community threat: " 'They seem to be targeting just about everyone except the folks who operate the tour boats on the Ottawa River' says Perrin Beatty, president and CEO of the CME [Canadian Manufacturers and Exporters]. 'What we're seeing is a group of well-fed, mainly white protesters from the developed world who want to spare the developing world of prosperity and growth' " (Mills and Agrell 2002, C3).

Similar messages appeared in local newspapers before each of the protests I studied. For example, a few days before the

2000 IMF/WB protests, the *Washington Times* reported that police had issued a "citizens advisory," stating that anarchists were calling for actions such as "trashing the inside of a retail chain store, smashing a McDonald's window, whacking a CEO [and] puncturing cop car tires. . . . Police said the anarchist organization, Fighting the Octopus/Global Action Against Capitalism, is using its Web site to call on the demonstrators to target people and establishments" (Taylor and Cella 2002, B1).

In New York, a WEF representative tried to make the movement look publicly dangerous: "If it's true these people are not willing to condemn violence, after all this city has been through, I think they should be ashamed of themselves. . . . I don't think New Yorkers will be very receptive to people who come here with violent intentions" (Pisik 2002, A9). The *New York Daily News* reported that police expected potentially violent groups to gather in the city. According to the paper, police had collected intelligence on various groups and had found that "one demonstration tactic labeled a serious threat, known as the 'Black Block,' is in vogue with anarchist groups. Demonstrators wear black clothing and bandannas over their faces, and wield pipes, bottles and Molotov cocktails" (O'Shaughnessy 2002, 10). A *New York Post* article reported that former New York City deputy police chief John Timoney was predicting "a potentially scary scene, promised by little nasty twits. . . . There are some very serious bad guys out there . . . and I am not talking about Osama bin Laden. We are talking about pretty sophisticated bad guys" (Dunleavy 2002, A8).[6]

In short, before each protest, the media reports that violent anarchists are coming to town, representing them as individuals likely to trash cities (Haberman 2002); throw rocks and hockey pucks (Bronskill 2002b); chuck urine, acid, and bleach on police (Nesmith 2003); and break store windows (Baker 2002). The vilification of the anarchists (and, by implication, the movement) is no coincidence. It is directly linked to what Claudia

Arandau (2001) and other scholars term *securitization*, which manufactures "a sudden rapture in the routinized, everyday life by fabricating an existential threat which provokes experience of the real possibility of violence and death." Securitization is all about securing and protecting citizens from a threat, which gives the state legitimacy to undertake extreme measures to protect itself and keep the larger citizenry secure. The terrorist attacks on the World Trade Center provided such a threat in 2001 and thus allowed police and global elites to connect the movement to terrorism. Each anti-globalization protest is now framed as a possible deadly threat, allowing the state to gather enormous resources and mitigate dissent.

The Chilling Effect

The chilling effect is the cooling off that can occur in a local community and within a movement. It is the result of a technology of control that produces fear. Local communities are afraid to aid or join the protests; many activists are afraid to attend a protest, and those that do are compliant and self-policing.

The chilling effect is the result of two factors. First, police vilify anarchists, repeatedly warning the community of possible violence. Second, they adopt a tough stand against the threat of violence, suggesting that they will use all their power to secure the safety of meeting delegates and the local population.

During telephone interviews with me, officers went out of their way to suggest that the role of the police at a protest is to protect the public and respect protesters' right to peacefully express their grievances. For instance, a lieutenant with the Washington, D.C., police stated that police received extensive training in "constitutional issues that surround protest, explaining that protestors have the right to protest under the First and Fourth Amendments to the Constitution. . . . . Police are there to provide service to protestors, not to stop them. We train our officers to provide service only, unless there is damage to property or injury to people." According to this discourse, the police are public servants, intermediaries between the public and the protesters. Yet when officers spoke about protesters, they also tended to make a sharp distinction between "good" (peaceful) and "bad" (violent) ones. This finding supports P.A.J. Waddington's (1999) research showing that British police officers tend to give more leeway to protesters they perceive as good. The threat of "bad" protesters allows police to respond with mass force. A review of newspaper coverage shows that, approximately two months before a protest, police adopt a harsh tone toward "violent" protesters while maintaining they will protect the rights of "peaceful" ones. They specifically post warnings of "zero tolerance" and "harsh punishment" for activists who cause trouble. For instance, a month before the WEF protests, Joseph Esposito with the New York City Police Department announced that a protester seeking to do violence should "go somewhere else . . . because we're going to take swift action against you. We're not going to tolerate any law breaking of any kind" (Mautot 2002). To back up the threat, the police said they would invoke an 1845 mask law (discussed elsewhere in this book) and ban backpacks. If any anarchist attempted to resist any law, he or she would be arrested immediately. The police chief even suggested that officers would arrest protesters if they so much as jaywalked.

The pattern of control is clear to those inside the movement. Laura, an anti–globalization activist with several years of experience in organizing protests, offered her perspective:

> The pattern of control . . . is a combination of two things. First, they tell stories to the public about the anarchists coming to town. Second, they tell about the terrorist things [anarchists] have done, such as throw acid and all that ridiculous stuff. Then they start to put fear on the city, interrupting things as usual, reporting to people that city and public services will be shut down, which makes people start to feel

nervous. Then they say things like "Don't come to work the day of the protests; shut down your business because it is going to be violent out here." A week or two before the protest they will start to show stories of some "incidents" of the coming protest. They will arrest some squatters, people making equipment; somebody will be arrested so that people know that it's starting. It will appear in the news a week before as an example of these bad protesters and why we need to be afraid. Finally, we see an increasing escalation of police in the streets as we lead into the protest. We see this every time.

I asked her about the cumulative effect of such actions. She said, "It makes people in the local community afraid of us. It indoctrinates the message that the protesters are bad and terrorist. It keeps the news away from the real substantive issues. It causes business to close down and keeps residents not only away from the businesses but also away from joining the protest. We call it the chilling effect. And the chilling effect is the intent to keep people from participating in the protest."

In the field I observed the chilling effect several times. In Cancun, for instance, I had several conversations with local people about the protests. Each individual expressed fears about the *globofobicos* in town. One middle-aged woman said, "It's getting so that I am afraid to be in the streets. You never know when these people will turn violent."[7] In Washington, D.C., I witnessed a restaurant owner yell at several activists, telling them to "go back where you came from. We don't want your trouble here." In Miami, the *Associated Press* reported that locals were terrified of the protests. " 'Everyone is scaring us. They say there's going to be trouble,' said [a resident], who was placing plywood in the window of his watch shop. . . . 'It's worse than a hurricane' " (Schneider 2003).

When the community has turned against the movement, activists have a hard time securing sleeping and meeting locations or food and material donations. In addition, they find it almost impossible to get the movement's message out to frightened local residents. Moreover, such "get tough" rhetoric produces layers of fear among activists that disrupt the movement itself. By distinguishing between "good" and "bad" protesters, law enforcement capitalizes on (and sometimes creates) internal strife between more established sections of the movement, such as labor unions and nongovernmental agencies, and more radical sections, such as groups that are likely to use direct action. I witnessed this fear in the faces and behavior of fellow activists in Arizona, who were intrigued about the movement but kept a safe distance because of the violent reputation of such protests.

In the end, however, it is up to protesters to see through the police rhetoric. And seeing through it is not enough. They also have to formulate new messages that release them from the violent anarchist frame and create a positive vision for a new world.

CHAPTER 7

Law Enforcement
and Control

In Multitude, Hardt and Negri (2004)
argue that modes of repression always follow innovations in resistance, not the other way around. They suggest that dissenters are
innovators, creating from necessity new ways to resist and challenge the status quo. The state then follows, implementing new
forms of control to mitigate challenges to its power. Affinity
groups, clusters, and direct action have formed a new constella-
tion of protest that has seriously challenged the agenda of large
globalization institutions such as the WTO and the IMF. In
response, the state, working closely with these institutions, has
developed new techniques to minimize potential disruption. As I
have shown throughout this book, these techniques included a
careful mapping and fortification of space as well as the use of
legal restraints and public relations campaigns. This spiral dance
requires constant change and assessment from social movement
activists who challenge the status quo. As Hardt and Negri would
predict, they must recognize new forms of policing and respond
with creative ways to resist and broadcast their message.
Otherwise, movements run the risk of becoming unimportant.

LEGAL, PHYSICAL, AND
PSYCHOLOGICAL CONTROL

Evidence suggests that movements now face increasingly
refined techniques of legal control. Through various agencies,

the state has employed legal mechanisms to inhibit mobilization. Temporary ordinances, creative use of old laws, and legal permits are now common ways to control protests. Yet while we know that law enforcement may use mass arrests to empty out streets and court cases to drain time and funds from activists organizations (Barkan 2001, 2004), we may overlook other forms of legal activity that operate at multiple levels and at different periods throughout the cycle of a single protest. Examples such as police data gathering before a protest, Miami's Street and Sidewalks Ordinance, and creative use of city fire codes point to a microlevel of legal regulation that we must study further.

Evidence also suggests that physical control of a large anti-globalization protest starts months before the actual event. This implies that we must look at how police plan and prepare for such large gatherings, yet analysis of police preparation goes mostly ignored in both the policing and social movement literatures. When we look at such planning processes, however, we find that police are moving to confront network-based movements that are nimble in the streets. Hence, control of space becomes a central factor. As we have seen, police have used geography to separate protesters from ministers and representatives. In other cases, they have mapped entire sections of cities and assigned undercover agents to monitor crowd movement. The important point is not the specific tactic but the way in which law enforcement has enclosed, zoned off, and militarized space to deal with the diffuse nature of the anti-globalization movement.

Finally, police use psychological means to control dissent. Disciplinary mechanisms can induce specific feelings in activists and the public regarding the nature of protest itself. For instance, law enforcement agencies use detailed public relations campaigns to frame the movement as violent and anarchist, their primary goal being to isolate protesters and produce unfavorable media coverage.

Thoughts on the Characteristics of the State and Policing

Study of the policing of the anti-globalization movement shows that the state can adapt quickly to a changing repertoire of contention. At a broader level, however, my findings suggest that the state plays a more complicated role in globalization than the literature currently describes. One debate in that literature centers around whether or not the state is weakening because of globalization. Scholars argue that, in the late twentieth century, we saw an increasingly faster pace and intensity of global interconnection (Harvey 1989; Bauman 1998; Castells 2000; Hardt and Negri 2000, 2004). Driven primarily by capitalism, this quickening occurred simultaneously with a communication technology explosion that transformed how we work, produce, and consume. Scholars postulate that these changes meant that the state, as conceptualized by early and mid-twentieth-century thinkers, no longer existed (Ohmae 1995, Held and McGrew 2000). Global institutions such as the WTO would soon take over significant territorial and legal powers, and at the very least the nation-state would no longer enjoy its customary independence.

It is indisputable that new global regulatory bodies can now overrule decisions reached at the national level. Yet while mounting data point to the increasing power of globacracies, my research highlights a different trend. In regard to the social control of dissent, the state is not disappearing. In fact, it may be gaining strength as it works with globacracies.

The state today is in flux, allowing larger bodies to regulate trade while remaining deeply entrenched in the business of security. When neoliberalist ideas took hold in the 1990s, state managers, in collusion with capitalist elites and the corporate world, created supranational institutions to open up markets across the world. Although the state gave up certain regulatory powers over commerce to institutions such as the WTO, it kept the legitimacy to violence. My evidence shows that the Canadian, U.S., and Mexican governments have spent a great amount of money and resources in securing and protecting globacracies. Therefore, we as scholars must keep the state central in our analysis.

IMPLICATIONS FOR THE
NEGOTIATED MANAGEMENT MODEL

During the past decade, scholars have developed a body of literature around the policing of protest (McCarthy and McPhail 1997, della Porta and Reiter 1998, Waddington 1999). Central is the contention that a shift occurred in the 1960s in the policing of protest in western democracies: from an intolerant, escalated-force style to a more tolerant, softer, negotiated management model (della Porta and Reiter 1998). According to McCarthy and McPhail (1997), this model relies on law enforcement's respect for the First Amendment. Police negotiate with protesters to preserve the right of speech while maintaining a secure and safe street demonstration. Toward this end, they apply city-imposed permit requirements that regulate the scale, route, and timing of demonstrations; respond to protests by force or negotiation based on the characteristics of protesters, targets, and tactics (della Porta and Reiter 1998, McPhail et al. 1998); and alternate between tolerance and repression based on their familiarity with the groups participating (Waddington 1998). In other words, police may tolerate some protesters but not others (della Porta and Reiter 1998, Waddington 1999).

These scholars, then, explain that police behavior is based on some perceived, inherent quality in the protesters, implying a scenario in which police use either repression or tolerance, force or negotiation. This juxtaposition is problematic because it does not help us understand how or when police use different techniques of control. In practice, they use both negotiation and force in targeted ways. For instance, at the WEF protest in

New York City, the police negotiated march routes with more mainstream groups while targeting the anarchist Black Block with repressive control techniques during the permitted march. Clearly, negotiated approaches and force co-exist and complement one another; and the negotiated management model in fact may mask how permits and police negotiations actually regulate, pacify, and control dissent.

SPACE, PROTEST, AND CONTROL

Protest is by necessity a public endeavor. It requires large numbers of people and big spaces to hold them. As Don Mitchell (2003) points out, protest usually occurs in public spaces regulated by the state to control and minimize the impact of dissenting citizens. While Mitchell looks specifically at the homeless population, his insights are relevant to understanding how the state controls and regulates the anti-globalization movement.

In the 1980s, because constitutional constraints did not allow it to control protesters' speech, the state began to regulate the time, duration, and location of protests (della Porta and Reiter 1998, McPhail et al. 1998, Mitchell 2003).[1] In the wake of several Supreme Court decisions, cities and states started requiring protesters to seek permits for public assembly, claiming that such permits were primarily intended to keep both the public and protesters from harm. As a result, some movements in the late 1980s and early 1990s adopted a protest repertoire that included symbolic and negotiated arrests. In other words, permits led to the rationalization of protest; and protest itself became predictable and habitual.

In the mid- to late 1990s new movements emerged with a different and more confrontational repertoire of protest, which included disruptive tactics and decentralized modes of organizing. Regulation of space through negotiation and permit requirements became less useful in controlling such anarchist-based movements. Therefore, the state adopted and implemented other forms of control that also focused on space, albeit in a different fashion.

Foucault's insights on disciplinary diagrams provide a framework for understanding how police map space to control a decentralized movement. Looking at historical cases, Foucault describes two models of control. The first targeted individuals suffering from leprosy, the second people infected with the plague. Leprosy, according to Foucault, was treated with banishment and isolation. The plague required a more complicated control technique. Unlike leprosy, the plague is highly contagious, with infection rates growing exponentially. To control it, the state developed what Foucault calls disciplinary diagrams: it portioned spaced into a grid and used surveillance and regular inspection (Elden 2003). Once a case was identified, a city magistrate would isolate or quarantine an individual house, thus suppressing the spread of the disease.

When looking at the policing of the anti-globalization movement, we notice a similar pattern. Across my five case studies, the police used what might be called the leprosy model in more rural areas and the plague model in more urban settings. For instance, in Calgary and Cancun, the police were able to use geography to their advantage, isolating protesters in areas far from the meetings, much as lepers were isolated on islands. In New York City, Washington, D.C., and Miami, the police resorted to plague-control methods. Before the FTAA protest, officers in Miami asked residents to remain at home, emptying the downtown of regular citizens. They mapped out the urban setting and placed heavy surveillance on all downtown streets, and they assembled a centralized system of information and employed small mobile police units to target protesters conducting actions at the affinity-group level. Once captured, protesters were banished to holding pens for the remainder of the protest.

7–1. Second perimeter police fence in Cancun, located nine miles from the 2003 WTO meetings. (Photograph by Luis Fernandez and Sue Hilderbrand)

Thus, we see police adopting methods of control that were previously used to prevent the biological spread of disease. The reason becomes obvious when we envision these protests as organic manifestations of the multitude. When dealing with nonhierarchical, network-based movements, police must devise policing strategies that deal with the spread of dissent.

HOPE AND INNOVATION

The policing of the anti-globalization movement bears witness to the cycle of resistance and innovation that Hardt and Negri (2004) describe. It is a dance between those who challenge authority, speak truth to power, and hope for a more just world and those who wish to extend their privilege and power. As Hardt and Negri suggest, the cycle starts with innovation, new forms of organizing, and waves of challenge to the state.

The state follows with countermoves, analysis, and the application of the logic of control. But we most not forget that this is only half the story.

My focus on control may have left the reader believing that the power of law enforcement is insurmountable. This is far from true. While tactics of control have indeed had devastating consequences on movements, they do not always succeed in stopping social change. The push and pull of control and resistance always tips to the side of justice, even though progress may seem to move at a glacial pace. In the case of the anti-globalization movement, new forms of protest brought not only new forms of control but also succeeded in opening the eyes of the world to the problem of corporate globalization. It gave legitimacy to the many voices that argued that global free trade was producing greater inequality and reducing democracy; and as a result, several nations have pulled out of large global negotiations. This counts as a success, even amid the growing control of dissent. At its best, the innovations of the anti-globalization movement will inspire another generation of young activists. Its work reminds us that resistance always lies just beneath the surface, waiting to rise when least expected. This gives me hope for the future.

Notes

Chapter 1 Protest, Control, and Policing

1. There are many names for the anti-globalization movement. Some call it the *anti-corporate globalization movement* to draw attention to a critical, anti-capitalist opposition. Others call it the *global justice movement*, highlighting its social justice ideals, such as fighting for debt reduction for impoverished nations. Yet others refer to it as the *movement of movements* to emphasize the wide scope of the struggle and the numerous grievances throughout in the world. *Alterglobalization*, an increasingly popular term, addresses the critique that the movement is only oppositional and presents no alternative. While any of these terms would suffice, I use *anti-globalization* to pay respect to the movement's confrontational and anti-capitalist aspects.
2. By the state, I mean the larger apparatus of government that includes law enforcement agencies as well as federal, county, and city governments.
3. By the social control of dissent, I mean those social control mechanisms associated primarily with control of social movements, street protest, and general challenges to the state. It excludes all the other social control mechanisms that also exist in society.
4. Contemporary examples of this tactic include the trials of Leonard Peltier, Mumia Abu-Jamal, Nelson Mandela, and the Chicago Seven after the Democratic National Convention.
5. *Verstehen* describes an approach to knowledge that requires compassion and deep connection with those one studies. I explain the concept further in this chapter.

Chapter 2 Perspectives on the Control of Dissent

1. While both political scientists and sociologists look at social control in movements, sociologists have done the majority of the work on the topic.
2. The work of these scholars is an approach that seeks to understand control rather than an existing school of thought.

3. Hardt and Negri (2004) make it clear that immaterial labor constitutes only a small part of the world economy and is mostly concentrated in the developed nations. In other words, the existence of immaterial labor does not mean that material labor has disappeared. Rather, the appearance of immaterial labor is changing how all other labor is managed. After all, when Marx described the changes that industrialization was bringing to worldwide social relations, industrialization was concentrated in what were then developing counties and was only a small section of the entire global economy.

4. The common should not be confused with the commons. The term *commons* is associated with precapitalist shared space that is now gone. The common is a look toward the future, not a turn to the past.

5. *Rhizome* is a biological term for a rootlike stem that grows horizontally under or along the ground and sends out roots from its lower surface and leafy shoots from its upper surface. Deleuze and Guattari (1988) borrow the term to describe systems that have no center or hierarchy and work primarily by circular logic.

6. Globacracies are global bureaucratic institutions (such as the WTO) that enforce the corporate global agenda and neoliberal policies. In this book I use *globacracies* and *global bureaucratic institutions* interchangeably.

7. Snatch squads are small police units trained to snatch groups or individuals from the middle of an ongoing march (see Chapter 5).

CHAPTER 3   THE ANTI-GLOBALIZATION MOVEMENT

1. Activists often refer to the 1999 WTO protest in Seattle, Washington, as the Battle of Seattle. I will use both references interchangeably.

2. In urban Spain, affinity groups formed around the same or similar crafts, with an emphasis on locality and diversity. In rural areas, locality was the primary basis of organization (Bookchin 1977).

3. This regional model is experiencing a revival in North America. There are several anarchist federations forming in various regions of North America, including the North American Federation of Anarcho-Communists.

4. Street medics are activists with medical backgrounds who administer first aid to protesters during an event.

5. Not every affinity group joins a cluster. In practice, many groups work autonomously.

6. Both quotations are from announcements made at a spokescouncil meeting during the 2003 WEF protest in New York City.

7. The interaction between the anti-globalization and the anti-war movements was interesting and complicated. Many activists who had gained experience at anti-globalization gatherings were also participating in the anti-war marches and rallies. But the anti-war

movement also drew in older activists with experience in the anti-nuclear and peace movements of the 1980s and 1990s. These individuals were not necessarily familiar with the values or tactics of the anti-globalization movement, which produced conflicts over how to organize protests and use street tactics. While not directly connected to my current research, this clash was part of the context of the post–September 11 organizing milieu.

CHAPTER 4 MANAGING AND REGULATING PROTEST

1. The full name is the Miami Streets and Sidewalks Ordinance, no. 12430, sec. 54-6.1.
2. There is evidence that meeting planners for global institutions such as the WTO and the WEF are selecting cities with little history of local activism and few organic organizations, which makes the process of organizing an international protest difficult. This was the case when the WTO selected Qatar (2001) and Cancun (2003). The WEF chose to meet in New York shortly after September 11, hoping to minimize protesters' ability to organize in a city that had just experienced trauma.
3. It seems only fair to mention that, during the 2000 Democratic National Convention in Los Angeles, seventy activists reportedly suffered illnesses that may have been related to unsanitary food handling by Food Not Bombs activists. To my knowledge, however, thousands of other meals have been served by the organization without incident.

CHAPTER 5 THIS IS WHAT DEMOCRACY LOOKS LIKE?

1. Two weeks before the 2004 G8 protests in Georgia, the governor, citing a potential terrorist threat, declared a state of emergency around the location where the leaders of the most powerful countries would meet, which opened the door to federal funding. I was unable, however, to learn exactly how much money the state received.
2. The Counter Intelligence Program (COINTELPRO) was an FBI effort to disrupt dissent among political organizations in the 1960s and 1970s. The program was discovered only after individuals broke into an FBI office and stole what came to be known as the COIN-TELPRO papers.
3. For a detailed description of the effects of the USA PATRIOT Act on political dissent, see Chang (2002).
4. The Direct Action Network is a loose network of anarchists and anti-authoritarians that promote direct action. The groups organized for and at the 1999 WTO protest in Seattle. By 2002, groups from that anti-globalization movement were joining forces with anti-war

groups. Perhaps the infiltration of the groups mentioned here was partly aided by a fear that these groups could successfully merge.

5. In fact, spokescouncil activities were reported in the *New York Times* throughout the week.

6. Koreans farmers played a central role in the Cancun protests, where the central topic of discussion at the WTO was global agriculture. On September 10, 2003, Lee Kyang Hae, a Korean farmer and head of South Korea's Federation of Farmers and Fishermen, stabbed himself in the heart to protest against the WTO. He died in a Mexican hospital shortly after the incident.

7. *French barricades* are what the officer called them during an interview with me.

Chapter 6   "Here Come the Anarchists"

1. Miami Police Chief John Timoney claims to have embedded two reporters during the 2000 Republican National Convention, when he was working in Philadelphia. See La Corte (2003) for more details.

2. The civil rights group Save Our Liberties provided me with a copy of the police presentation entitled "Miami Police: FTAA." When asked about the presentation, police public relations officers declined to comment. The presentation bears the logo of the Miami-Dade Police Department.

3. For further discussion on the meaning of *anarchist* from an anarchist perspective, see Guerin (1970) or Wolff (1976).

4. Because Mexico's historical context differs from that of the United States, the meanings that surround protest also differ. Here we see the state claiming that protesters stand in the way of Mexican economic development.

5. Empirical evidence suggests that a movement's relationship to violence is more complicated than Buttel and Gould (2004) propose. Gamson (1997) argues that social movements that embrace violence actually have an above-average rate of success.

6. Timoney has a notorious history with the anti-globalization movement. He was in charge of policing the 2000 National Democratic Convention in Philadelphia, where hundreds were arrested and activists complained of police brutality. He was also in charge of the Miami police during the now infamous 2003 Miami FTAA protest, known for its high level of police brutality.

7. I translated this quotation from Spanish.

Chapter 7   Law Enforcement and Control

1. For a detailed analysis of the effect of Supreme Court cases on public space, see Mitchell (2003).

BIBLIOGRAPHY

American Civil Liberties Union. 2003. ACLU urges Miami officials to revise unconstitutional ordinance aimed at limiting protest during free trade meetings. Press release, September 24.

Amster, R. 2004. *Street people and the contested realms of public space.* New York: LFB Scholarly Publishers.

Appadurai, A. 1996. *Modernity at large: Cultural dimensions of globalization.* Minneapolis: University of Minnesota Press.

————. 2001. *Globalization.* Durham, N.C.: Duke University Press.

Aradau, C. 2001. Beyond good and evil: Ethics and securitization/desecuritization techniques. *Rubikon.* Retrieved on May 2, 2006, from *http://venus.ci.uw.edu.pl/~rubikon/forum/claudia2.htm.*

Armond, P. D. 2001. Netwar in the Emerald City: WTO protest strategy and tactics. In *Networks and netwars: The future of terror, crime, and militancy,* edited by D. F. Ronfeldt, 201–35. Santa Monica, Calif.: Rand.

Art and Revolution. 2004. Art and revolution convergence. Retrieved on March 17, 2004, from *http://www.groundworknews.org/culture/culture-artrevol.html.*

Atterton, P. 1994. Power's blind struggle for existence: Foucault, genealogy and Darwinism. *History of the Human Sciences* 7, no. 4: 1–20.

Atton, C. 2003. Reshaping social movement media for a new millennium. *Social Movement Studies* 2, no. 1: 3–15.

Ayres, J. M. 2004. Framing collective action against neoliberalism: The case of the "anti-globalization" movement. *Journal of World-Systems Research* 10, no. 1: 11–34.

Baker, A. 2002. Conference neighborhoods start preparing for strife: Forum draws a different kind of visitor. *New York Times,* January 30, 2002, p. A29.

Balbus, I. D. 1973. *The dialectics of legal repression: Black rebels before the American criminal courts.* New York: Sage Foundation.

Barkan, S. E. 1984. Legal control of southern civil rights movements. *American Sociological Review* 49, no. 4: 552–65.

————. 2001. Legal repression and social movements. Paper presented at the annual meeting of the American Sociological Association, Washington, D.C., August 17–19.

———. 2004. Criminal prosecution and trial: A neglected dynamic in the study of social movements. Paper presented at the annual meeting of the American Sociological Association, San Francisco, August 14–17.

Barlow, M., and T. Clarke. 2002. *Blue gold: The fight to stop the corporate theft of the world's water.* New York: New Press.

Bauman, Z. 1998. *Globalization: The human consequences.* New York: Columbia University Press.

Beck, U. 2000. *What is globalization?* Cambridge, U.K.: Polity.

Becker, H. S. 1963. *Outsiders: Studies in the sociology of deviance.* London: Free Press of Glencoe.

Bello, W. F., and A. Mittal. 2001. *The future in the balance: Essays on globalization and resistance.* Oakland, Calif.: Food First Books.

Benford, R. D. 1993a. Frame disputes within the nuclear disarmament movement. *Social Forces* 71: 677–701.

———. 1993b. "You could be the hundredth monkey": Collective action frames and vocabularies of motive within the nuclear disarmament movement. *Sociology Quarterly* 34: 195–216.

Benford, R. D., and D. A. Snow. 2000. Framing processes and social movements: An overview and assessment. *Annual Review of Sociology* 26: 611–39.

Berkman, A. 1971. *A.B.C. of anarchism.* London: Freedom Press.

———. 2003. *What is anarchism?* Oakland, Calif.: AK Press.

Black Cross Health Collective. 2004. Web page. Retrieved on April 12, 2004, from *http://blackcrosscollective.org.*

Blomberg, T. G., and S. Cohen. 2003. *Punishment and social control.* New York: Aldine de Gruyter.

Blumner, R. E. 2003. Miami crowd control would do tyrant proud. *St. Petersburg Times*, November 30, 2003, p. 1.

Bookchin, M. 1977. *The Spanish anarchists: The heroic years, 1868–1936.* New York: Free Life Editions.

Bourdieu, P. 1984. *Distinction: A social critique of the judgment of taste.* Cambridge, Mass., Harvard University Press.

Brecher, J., T. Costello, and B. Smith. 2000. *Globalization from below: The power of solidarity.* Cambridge, Mass.: South End Press.

Bronskill, J. 2002a. Anarchists planning G8 attacks: Activists says spy agency is trying to "demonize" protesters. *Ottawa Citizen*, June 2, 2002, p. A3.

———. 2002b. Militant anarchists expected. *Calgary Herald*, April 27. Retrieved on June 12, 2007, from *http://www.geocities.com/eriesquire/articles/calher042702b.htm.*

Burawoy, M. 1998. The extended case method. *Social Theory* 16, no. 1: 4–33.

———. 2000. Introduction: Reaching for the global. In *Global ethnography: Forces, connections, and imaginations in a postmodern world*, edited by M. Burawoy, 1–40. Berkeley: University of California Press.

Butler, C. T. L., and K. McHenry. 2000. *Food not bombs*. Tucson: See Sharp Press.

Buttel, F., and K. A. Gould. 2004. Global social movement(s) at the crossroads: Some observations on the trajectory of the anti-globalization movement. *Journal of World-System Research* 10, no. 1: 11–24.

California Commission on Peace Officer Standards and Training. 2003. Crowd management and civil disobedience guidelines.

Carlson, C. 2003. Amnesty International, protesters call for investigation of police action during trade talks. *Associated Press*, November 27, 2003.

Castells, M. 2000. *The rise of the network society*. Oxford: Blackwell.

Cavanagh, J. 2002. The history of the movement. Retrieved on November 21, 2004, from *http://www.fpif.org/discussion/0201globalization/messages/4.html*.

Cavanagh, J., J. Mander, S. Anderson, D. Barker, M. Barlow, W. Bello, R. Broad, T. Clarke, E. Goldsmith, R. Hayes, C. Hines, A. Kimbrell, D. Korten, H. Norberg-Hodge, S. Larrain, S. Retallack, V. Shiva, V. Tauli-Corpuz, and L. Wallach. 2002. *Alternatives to economic globalization: A better world is possible*. San Francisco: Berrett-Koehler.

Chang, N. 2002. *Silencing political dissent*. New York: Seven Stories Press.

Chapman, D. 2003. Free Trade Area of the Americas, stumbling blocks remain. *Atlanta Journal-Constitution*, October 30, 2003, p. A5.

Churchill, W. 2001. "To disrupt, discredit, and destroy": The FBI's secret war against the Black Panther Party. In *Liberation, imagination, and the Black Panther Party: A new look at the panthers and their legacy*, edited by G. N. Katsiaficas, 78–119. New York: Routledge.

———. 2002. *In a pig's eye: Reflections on the police state, repression, and Native America*. Oakland, Calif.: AK Press.

Churchill, W., and J. Vander Wall. 2002. *Agents of repression: The FBI's secret wars against the Black Panther Party and the American Indian movement*. Cambridge, Mass.: South End Press.

City of Miami Police Department. 2003. Slide presentation.

———. 2004. FTAA: After action review.

Cohen, A. K. 1966. *Deviance and control*. Englewood Cliffs, N.J., Prentice Hall.

Davenport, C., H. Johnston, and C. M. Mueller. 2004. *Repression and mobilization*. Minneapolis: University of Minnesota Press.

Deleuze, G., and F. Guattari. 1988. *A thousand plateaus: Capitalism and schizophrenia*. London: Athlone.

Deleuze, G., and S. Hand. 1988. *Foucault*. Minneapolis: University of Minnesota Press.

della Porta, D. 1998. Police knowledge and protest policing: Some reflections on the Italian case. In *Policing of protest: The control of the mass demonstration in western democracies*, edited by D. della Porta and H. Reiter, 228–52. Minneapolis: University of Minnesota Press.

———. 1999. Protest, protesters, and protest policing: Public discourses in Italy and Germany from the 1960s to the 1980s. In *How social movements matter*, edited by D. M. Marco Giugni and C. Tilly, 66–96. Minneapolis: University of Minnesota Press.

della Porta, D., and M. Diani. 1999. *Social movements: An introduction*. Oxford: Blackwell.

della Porta, D., and H. Reiter, eds. 1998. *Policing protest: The control of mass demonstrations in western democracies*. Minneapolis: University of Minnesota Press.

della Porta, D., and S. Tarrow. 2001. After Genoa and New York: The antiglobal movement, the police and terrorism. In *Items and Issues* 2, nos. 3–4: 9–11.

Dunleavy, S. 2002. Econ summit brings own terror threat. *New York Post*, January 18, 2002, p. A8.

Earl, J. 2003. Tanks, tear gas, and taxes: Toward a theory of movement repression. *Sociological Theory* 21, no. 1: 44–68.

Earl, J., S. A. Soule, and J. D. McCarthy. 2003. Protest under fire? Explaining the policing of protest. *American Sociological Review* 68: 581–606.

Elden, S. 2003. Plague, panopticon, police. *Surveillance and Society* 1, no. 3: 240–53.

Epstein, B. 2001. Anarchism and the anti-corporate globalization movement. *Monthly Review* 53, no. 3: 1–14.

Equipo Rumbo a Cancun. 2004. Call to mobilize against the WTO in Cancun. Retrieved on December 11, 2004, from *http://www.nadir.org/nadir/initiativ/agp/free/cancun/0515callcancun.htm*.

Ericson, R., and A. Doyle. 1999. Globalization and the policing of protest: The case of APEC 1997. *British Journal of Sociology* 50, no. 4: 589–608.

Fahrenthold, D. A. 2002. D.C. police struggle to staff IMF protests; outside agencies hesitate. *Washington Post*, August 27, p. B01.

Ferree, M. M. 2004. Soft repression: Ridicule, stigma, and silencing in gender-based movements. In *Repression and mobilization*, edited by C. M. Mueller, 276–98. Minneapolis: University of Minnesota Press.

Ferrell, J., and M. S. Hamm. 1998. *Ethnography at the edge: Crime, deviance, and field research*. Boston: Northeastern University Press.

Foucault, M. 1973. *The order of things: An archaeology of the human sciences*. New York: Vintage.

———. 1979. *Discipline and punish: The birth of the prison*, translated by A. Sheridan. New York: Vintage.

———. 1983. The subject and the power. In *Michel Foucault: Beyond structuralism and hermeneutics*, edited by H. L. Dreyfus and P. Rabinow, 208–28. Chicago: University of Chicago Press.

———. 1988. *The history of sexuality*, translated by R. Hurley. New York: Vintage.

Foucault, M., L. H. Martin, H. Gutman, and P. H. Hutton. 1988. *Technologies of the self: A seminar with Michel Foucault*. Amherst: University of Massachusetts Press.

Fowler, C. 1995. Biotechnology, patents, and the Third World. In *Biopolitics: A feminist and ecological reader on biotechnology*, edited by V. Shiva and I. Moser, 214–25. London: Zed.

Frank, A. G. 1998. *Reorient: Global economy in the Asian age*. Berkeley: University of California Press.

Fung, A., D. O'Rourke, C. F. Sabel, J. Cohen, and J. Rogers. 2001. *Can we put an end to sweatshops?* Boston: Beacon.

Galvan, L. 2004. Peace Fresno files complaint, now-deceased deputy is accused of infiltrating group. *Fresno Bee*, April 22, 2004, p. B1.

Gamson, W. A. 1990. *The strategy of social protest*. Belmont, Calif.: Wadsworth.

———. 1997. The success of the unruly. In *Social movements: Readings on their emergence, mobilization, and dynamics*, edited by D. A. Snow, 357–66. Los Angeles: Roxbury.

Gamson, W. A., B. Fireman, and S. Rytina. 1982. *Encounters with unjust authority*. Homewood, Ill.: Dorsey.

Garland, D. 1990. *Punishment and modern society: A study in social theory*. Chicago: University of Chicago Press.

Gillham, P., and G. Marx. 2000. Complexity and irony in policing and protesting: The world trade organization in Seattle. *Social Justice* 27, no. 2: 212–36.

Giugni, M., D. McAdam, and C. Tilly. 1999. *How social movements matter*. Minneapolis: University of Minnesota Press.

Glaser, B. G., and A. L. Strauss. 1968. *The discovery of grounded theory: Strategies for qualitative research*. London: Weidenfeld and Nicolson.

Goldman, E., and R. Drinnon. 1969. *Anarchism and other essays*. New York: Dover.

Goode, E. 2001. *Deviant behavior*. Upper Saddle River, N.J.: Prentice Hall.

Guerin, W. 1970. *Anarchism*, translated by M. Klopper. New York: Monthly Review Press.

Haberman, C. 2002. NYC; with thanks comes a call for restraint. *New York Times*, January 19, 2001, p. B1.

Hardt, M., and A. Negri. 2000. *Empire*. Cambridge, Mass.: Harvard University Press.

———. 2004. *Multitude: War and democracy in the age of empire*. New York: Penguin.

Harvey, D. 1989. *The condition of postmodernity: An enquiry into the origins of cultural change*. Oxford: Blackwell.

Hayden, T. 2002. *The Zapatista reader*. New York: Thunder's Mouth/Nation Books.

———. 2003. Miami vice. Retrieved on November 20, 2003, from *http://www.alternet.org/story.html?StoryID=17234*.

Heckscher, Z. 2002. Long before Seattle: Historical resistance to economic globalization. In *Global backlash: Citizen initiatives for a just world economy*, edited by B. Broad, 86–91. Lanham, Md.: Rowman and Littlefield.

Held, D., and A. G. McGrew, eds. 2000. *The global transformations reader: An introduction to the globalization debate*. Malden, Mass.: Polity.

Hier, S. P. 2003. Probing the surveillant assemblage: On the dialectics of surveillance practices as processes of social control. *Surveillance and Society* 1, no. 3: 339–411.

Hirsh, S. 2003. Miami braces for trade protest. *Baltimore Sun*, November 19, 2003, p. 1A.

Hobbes, T. 1991. *Leviathan*, edited by R. Tuck. New York: Cambridge University Press.

Houtart, F., and F. Polet. 2001. *The other Davos summit: The globalization of resistance to the world economic system*. New York: Zed.

Hovey, A. 2003. Assistant DA's job might be in jeopardy, her attorney says. *Albuquerque Tribune*, March 27, 2003, p. A6.

Jimenez, O. J., and F. Reinares. 1998. The policing of mass demonstrations in Spain: From dictatorship to democracy. In *Policing protest: The control of mass demonstrations in western democracies*, edited by D. della Porta and H. Reiter, 166–87. Minneapolis: University of Minnesota Press: 302.

Juris, J. 2005. The new digital media and activist networking within anti-corporate globalization movement. *Annals of the Academy of Political and Social Science* 597, no. 1: 119–208.

Katsiaficas, G. N. 1997. *The subversion of politics: European autonomous social movements and the decolonization of everyday life*. Atlantic Highlands, N.J.: Humanities Press.

Keohane, R. O., and J. S. Nye. 2000. Globalization: What's new? What's not? (And so what?). In *Power and interdependence*, edited by R. O. Keohane and J. S. Nye, 104–20. New York: Longman.

Kimbrell, A. 2002. *Fatal harvest: The tragedy of industrial agriculture*. Washington, D.C.: Foundation for Deep Ecology/Island Press.

King, M., and D. Waddington. 2004. Coping with disorder? The changing relationship between police public order strategy and practice: A critical analysis of the Burnley riot. *Policing and Society* 14, no. 2: 118–37.

———. 2005. Flashpoint revisited: A critical application to the policing of the anti-globalization protest. *Policing and Society* 15, no. 2: 255–82.

Kirchheimer, O. 1980. *Political justice: The use of legal procedure for political ends.* Westport, Conn.: Greenwood.

Kirton, J. 2004. *Explaining G8 effectiveness: A concert of vulnerable equals in a globalizing world.* Paper presented at the annual convention of the International Studies Association, Montreal, March 17–20.

Klein, N. 2000. *No logo: Taking aim at the brand bullies.* New York: Picador.

———. 2003. America's enemy within: Armed checkpoints, embedded reporters in flak jackets, brutal suppression of peaceful demonstrators. Baghdad? No, Miami. *Guardian,* November 24, 2003, p. 25.

Kofman, E., and G. Youngs. 2003. *Globalization: Theory and practice.* London: Continuum.

Kraska, P. 1997. Militarizing American police: The rise of paramilitary units. *Social Problems* 44, no. 1: 1–18.

———, ed. 2001. *Militarizing the American criminal justice system: The changing roles of the armed forces and the police.* Boston: Northeastern University Press.

La Corte, R. 2003. Media "embeds" with police as trade talks start. *Atlanta Journal-Constitution.* November 11, 2003.

Larsen, J. 2003. Securing support: Examining the success of the 2002 G8 summit security communication program. Report. Ottawa: GPC International.

Lauderdale, P., and M. Cruit. 1993. *The struggle for control: A study of law, disputes, and deviance.* Albany: State University of New York Press.

Leonnig, C. D. 2003. IMF arrests improper, police found; Ramsey memo acknowledges protesters weren't warned. *Washington Post,* September 13, p. B02.

Lianos, M. 2003. Social control after Foucault. *Surveillance and Society* 1, no. 3: 412–30.

Lichbach, M. 1987. Deterrence or escalation? The puzzle of aggregate studies of repression and dissent. *Journal of Conflict Resolution* 31: 266–97.

Lichtblau, E. 2005. F.B.I. watched activist groups, new files show. *New York Times,* December 20, 2005, p. A1.

Little, C. B. 1989. *Deviance and control: Theory, research, and social policy.* Itasca, Ill.: Peacock.

Lyon, D. 2002. *Surveillance society: Monitoring everyday life.* Buckingham, U.K.: Open University Press.

Main, F. 2004. Police infiltration of protest groups has civil rights activists fuming. *Chicago Sun-Times,* February 19, 2004, p. 26.

Marcus, G. E. 1995. Ethnography in/of the world system: The emergence of multi-sited ethnography. *Annual Review of Anthropology* 24: 95–117.

Marx, G. 1974. Thoughts on a neglected category of social movement participant: The agent provocateur and the informant. *American Journal of Sociology* 80: 402–42.

Marx, K. 1970. *An introduction to the critique of political economy*, edited by M. Dobb, translated by S. W. Ryazanskaya. New York: International.

——. 1977. *Capital: A critique of political economy*, translated by B. Fowkes. New York: Vintage.

Mautot, M. 2002. New York police promise zero tolerance for anti-Davos demonstrators. *Agence France Presse*, January 30, 2002.

McAdam, D. 1996. The framing function of movement tactics: Strategic dramaturgy in the American civil rights movement. In *Comparative perspectives on social movements: Political opportunities, mobilizing structures, and cultural framing*, edited by M. N. Zald, 338–55. Cambridge, U.K.: Cambridge University Press.

——. 1999. *Political process and the development of black insurgency, 1930–1970.* Chicago: University of Chicago Press.

McCarthy, J., and C. McPhail. 1997. The institutionalization of protest in the United States. In *The social movement society: Contentious politics for a new century*, edited by D. Meyer and S. Tarrow, 83–110. Boulder, Co.: Rowman and Littlefield.

McPhail, C., and J. McCarthy. 2005. Protest mobilization, protest repression, and their interactions. In *Repression and mobilization*, edited by C. Davenport, H. Johnston, C. M. Mueller, 3–32. Minneapolis: University of Minnesota Press.

McPhail, C., D. Schweingruber, and J. McCarthy. 1998. Policing protest in the United States, 1960–1995. In *Policing of protest: The control of the mass demonstration in western democracies*, edited by D. della Porta and H. Reiter, 49–69. Minneapolis: University of Minnesota Press.

Mertes, T., ed. 2004. *A movement of movements.* London: Verso.

Mikulan, S. 2002. A wintry discontent. *Los Angeles Weekly*, February 8, p. 28.

Mills, A. 2002. Militants aim to "take the capital": Groups plan mass protest for Ottawa to mark G8 summit. *Ottawa Citizen*, May 30, 2002, p. B1.

Mills, A., and S. Agrell. 2002. Guide to G8 protests outlines tactics: Police meet merchants, public to discuss security concerns. *Ottawa Citizen*, June 5, 2002, p. C3.

Mitchell, D. 2003. *The right to the city: Social justice and the fight for public space.* New York: Guilford.

Morris, A. D., and C. M. Mueller. 1992. *Frontiers in social movement theory.* New Haven, Conn.: Yale University Press.

Neocleous, M. 2000. *The fabrication of social order: A critical theory of police power.* Sterling, Va.: Pluto.

Nesmith, S. 2003. Police praise selves on absence of chaos: Police succeed in protecting downtown Miami from a small cadre of violent protesters, but activists groups complain of heavy-handed tactics. *Miami Herald*, November 29, 2003, p. A1.

————. 2004. Summit security costs public millions. *Miami Herald*, February 22, 2004, p. A1.

Noakes, J., and D. Sieminski. 2001. Beyond negotiated management: Transgressive contention and the police response to global justice protesters in three U.S. cities. Paper presented at the annual meeting of the American Sociological Association, Anaheim, Calif., August 17–19.

Noonan, R. K. 1995. Women against the state: Political opportunities and collective action frames in Chile's transition to democracy. *Sociological Forum* 10: 81–111.

Not in Our Name. 2004. Public statement, February 25.

Notes from Nowhere, ed. 2003. *We are everywhere: The irresistible rise of global anti-capitalism.* London: Verso.

Novak, B. 2003. Newby rips "police state." *Capital Times*, November 20, 2003, p. 14A.

Nye, J. S. 2001. Globalization's democratic deficit: How to make international institutions more accountable. *Foreign Affairs* 2, no. 6: 2–6.

Ohmae, K. 1995. *The end of the nation state: The rise of regional economies.* New York: Free Press.

O'Shaughnessy, P. 2002. Radicals to rally against the World Economic Forum in New York. *New York Daily News*, January 29, 2003, p. 10.

Panitch, L. 2002. Violence as a tool of order and change: The war on terrorism and the antiglobalization movement. *Monthly Review* 54, no. 2: 1–23.

Pertuiset, S., and J. Lemieux. 2002. Protesters prepare to camp out at Canadian Rockies venue for G8. *Agence France Presse*, June 25, 2002.

Pfohl, S. J. 1994. *Images of deviance and social control: A sociological history.* New York: McGraw-Hill.

Pisik, B. 2002. WEF foes won't nix violence in N.Y. *Washington Times*, January 16, 2002, p. A9.

Podobnik, B., and T. E. Riefer. 2004. The globalization protest movement in comparative perspective. *Journal of World-System Research* 10, no. 1: 3–9.

Police monitored anti-war rallies, chief says. 2004. *Associated Press*, March 28.

Public announcement by U.S. Department of State: G8 summit in Alberta creates potential for disruptions. 2002. *States News Service*, June 17.

Quinney, R. 2001. *The social reality of crime.* New Brunswick, N.J.: Transaction.

Rant Collective. 2004. Web page. Retrieved on October 2, 2004, from *http://rantcollective.org/article.php?id=30*.

Rasler, K. 1996. Concessions, repression, and political protest. *American Sociological Review* 61, no. 1: 132–52.

Ray, R. 1999. *Fields of protest: Women's movements in India.* Minneapolis: University of Minnesota Press.

Riccardi, N. 2006. F.B.I. keeps watch on activists; antiwar, other groups are monitored to curb violence, not because of ideology, agency says. *Los Angeles Times*, March 23, 2006, p. A1.

Rodriguez, V. 2003. Reporters to evaluate if Miami embed program was beneficial. Retrieved on January 14, 2004, from *http://www.rcfp.org/news/2003/1121journa.html#init.*

Rosenberg, G. N. 1991. *The hollow hope: Can courts bring about social change?* Chicago: University of Chicago.

Rubinstein, D. 2002. Canada preps for G8 summit. Retrieved on June 24, 2002, from *http://www.alternet.org/story/13446/.*

Sachs, J. 2000. International economics: Unlocking the mysteries of globalization. In *Globalization and the challenges of a new century: A reader*, edited by P. O'Meara, H. Mehlinger, and M. Krain, 217–26. Bloomington: Indiana University Press.

Salazar, C. 2004. Protest law headed toward repeal. *Miami Herald*, February 27, p. B2.

Sarup, M. 1993. *An introductory guide to post-structuralism and postmodernism.* Athens: University of Georgia Press.

Sassen, S. 1998. *Globalization and its discontents: Essays on the new mobility of people and money.* New York: New Press.

Scher, A. 2001. The crackdown on dissent. *Nation* 27, no. 5: 23–26.

Schneider, M. 2003. Security tight as FTAA protests increase in preparations for march. *Associated Press*, November 20, 2003.

Schweingruber, D. 2000. Mob sociology and escalated force: Sociology's contribution to repressive police tactics. *Sociological Quarterly* 41, no. 3: 371–89.

Secure culture basics. 2003. Pamphlet.

Shepard, B. H., and R. Hayduk. 2002. *From act up to the WTO: Urban protest and community building in the era of globalization.* London: Verso.

Shiller, R. 2001. *Irrational exuberance.* Princeton, N.J.: Princeton University Press.

Shiva, V. 1995. Biotechnological development and the conservation of biodiversity. In *Biopolitics: A feminist and ecological reader on biotechnology*, edited by V. Shiva and I. Moser, 193–213. London: Zed.

———. 1997. *Biopiracy: The plunder of nature and knowledge.* Boston: South End Press.

———. 2002. *Water wars: Privatization, pollution and profit.* Cambridge, Mass.: South End Press.

Shiva, V., and I. Moser, eds. 1995. *Biopolitics: A feminist and ecological reader on biotechnology.* London: Zed.

Smith, J. G., and H. Johnston. 2002. *Globalization and resistance: Transnational dimensions of social movements.* Lanham, Md., Rowman and Littlefield.

Snow, D. A., and R. D. Benford. 1988. Ideology, frame resonance, and participant mobilization. *International Social Movement Research* 1: 197–217.

———. 1992. Master frames and cycles of protest. In *Frontiers in social movement theory,* edited by C. M. Mueller, 133–55. New Haven, Conn.: Yale University Press.

Snow, D. A., E. B. Rochford, S. K. Worden, and R. D. Benford. 1986. Frame alignment processes, micromobilization, and movement participation. *American Sociological Review* 51: 464–81.

Starhawk. 2002a. How we really shut down the WTO. In *From act up to the WTO: Urban protest and community building in the era of globalization,* edited by B. H. Shepard and R. Hayduk, 52–56. New York: Verso.

———. 2002b. *Webs of power: Notes from the global uprising.* Gabriola, B.C.: New Society.

Starr, A. 2000. *Naming the enemy: Anti-corporate movements confront globalization.* New York: Zed.

Steier, F. 1991. *Research and reflexivity.* Newbury Park, Calif.: Sage.

Steward, L. 2001. Getting spooked: The anti-globalization movement is gaining momentum, but law enforcers are quickly catching up. *This Magazine* 34, no. 5: 24–28.

Stiglitz, J. E. 2002. *Globalization and its discontents.* New York: Norton.

———. 2003. Globalization and the economic role of the state in the new millennium. *Industrial and Corporate Change* 12, no. 1: 3–26.

Tarrow, S. G. 1989. *Democracy and disorder: Protest and politics in Italy, 1965–1975.* New York: Clarendon.

———. 1992. Mentalities, political cultures, and collective action frames: Constructing meanings through action. In *Frontiers in social movement theory,* edited by C. M. Mueller, 174–202. New Haven, Conn.: Yale University Press.

———. 1998. *Power in movement: Social movements and contentious politics.* Cambridge, U.K.: Cambridge University Press.

Taylor, G., and M. Cella. 2002. Police "advisory" targets vandals; cites urging of protest web site. *Washington Post,* September 24, 2002, p. B1.

Tilly, C. 1978. *From mobilization to revolution.* Reading, Mass.: Addison-Wesley.

Tracy, J. 1996. *Direct action: Radical pacifism from the Union Eight to the Chicago Seven.* Chicago: University of Chicago Press.

Travers, E. 2003. Cops tally hefty security costs: WTO tab unknown. Bills have soared since Seattle '99. *Gazette* [Montreal], August 8, 2003, p. A6.

U.S. Central Intelligence Agency. 2004. *The CIA world fact book on CD-ROM.* Washington, D.C.: U.S. Government Printing Office.

U.S. Department of Homeland Security. 2002. Hacktivism in connection with protest events of September 2002. Retrieved on June 28, 2004, from *http://www.nipc.gov/warnings/assessments/2002/02-002.htm.*

U.S. General Accounting Office. 2003. Free Trade Area of the Americas: Negotiations progress, but successful ministerial hinges on intensified U.S. preparations. Report. Washington, D.C., April.

Vahamaki, J. 2004. Controlling the multitude. *Ephemera* 4, no. 3: 233–45.

Waddington, D., K. Jones, and C. Critcher. 1989. *Flashpoints: Studies in public disorder.* London: Routledge.

Waddington, P.A.J. 1994. *Liberty and order: Public order policing in a capital city.* London: UCL Press.

———. 1998. Controlling protest in contemporary historical and comparative perspective. In *Policing protest: The control of mass demonstrations in western democracies,* edited by D. della Porta and H. Reiter, 117–42. Minneapolis: University of Minnesota Press.

———. 1999. *Policing citizens: Authority and rights.* London: UCL Press.

Weber, M., and E. A. Shils. 1949. *The methodology of the social sciences.* Glencoe, Ill.: Free Press.

Wisler, D., and M. Giugni. 1999. Under the spotlight: The impact of media attention on protest policing. *Mobilization* 4, no. 2: 171–87.

Wolff, R. P. 1976. *In defense of anarchism.* New York: Harper Colophon.

Wood, D. 2003. Editorial: Foucault and panopticism revisited. *Surveillance and Society* 1, no. 3: 234–239.

Woodroffe, J., and M. Ellis-Jones. 2000. *States of unrest.* London: World Development Movement.

World Economic Forum. 2004. Web page. Retrieved on March 12, 2004, from *http://www.weforum.org/.*

Wright, A. L., and W. Wolford. 2003. *To inherit the earth: The landless movement and the struggle for a new Brazil.* Oakland, Calif.: Food First Books.

Yuen, E., D. B. Rose, and G. Katsiaficas. 2001. *The Battle of Seattle: The new challenge to capitalist globalization.* New York: Soft Skull Press.

Zald, M. N. 1996. Culture, ideology and strategic framing. In *Comparative perspectives on social movements: Political opportunities, mobilizing structures, and cultural framings,* edited by M. N. Zald, 261–74. Cambridge, U.K.: Cambridge University Press.

INDEX

9/11/2001. *See* September 11, 2001

alterglobalization movement. *See* anti-globalization
anarcho-syndicalist movement, 11
anarchy, 51–55; 155–160; 176n3
anti-corporate globalization movement. *See* anti-globalization
anti-globalization: affinity group; 55–61, 174n5 (chap. 3); cultural, 42–43; economic, 43–46; movement, 15, 23, 30, 33, 37, 50, 52, 92, 173n1 (chap. 1); policing of networks, 6–7; political, 46–50
Arandau, Claudia, 160–161

Balbus, Isaac, 11
Barkan, Steven, 11
Battle of Seattle. *See* World Trade Organization (WTO) protests
Benford, Robert, 139, 156
biopiracy, 45
biopower, 25, 27. *See also* Foucault, Michel
Blomberg, Thomas, 19
Blumer, Herbert, 21

Bourdieu, Pierre, 32, 33
Burgess, Ernest N., 21

capitalism, 29, 31, 43, 155, 167
Cavanagh, John, 44
Chicago School of Sociology, 21
chilling effect, 161–164
Churchill, Ward, 11, 12, 108
clusters, 58–59, 174n5 (chap. 3)
Cohen, Stanley, 19
common, the, 30–31, 174n4 (chap.3)
commons, the, 174n4 (chap. 3)
conflict theory, 22
control: legal, 10–11, 72, 88–91, 165–166; physical, 92–137, 166; psychological, 138–164, 166

deviance, 21–24
Doyle, Aaron, 96

Earl, Jennifer, 8–9
Ericson, Richard, 96
escalated force model, 12

Federal Bureau of Investigation (FBI), 9, 106, 108–110, 175n2 (chap. 5)
Ferree, Myra Marx, 10
field of protest, 33
flashpoint model, 7–8

Food Not Bombs (FNB), 4–5, 80

Foucault, Michel: anonymity and aim of reducing in protest, 119; biopower, 16, 24–25; disciplinary diagrams, 170; government, 26; governmentality, 16, 24–26; organization of labor, 27; power mechanisms, 130; power (or domination), 24; social control, 24, 130; technological control, 24–25

frames: bridging, 157; collective action, 139, 146; concept of, 138–139; strategic process, 156; violent anarchist, 156–161

Free Trade Area of the Americas (FTAA), 45, 47, 68, 152–153. *See also* Free Trade Area of the Americas (FTAA) protests

Free Trade Area of the Americas (FTAA) protests, 68–72, 88, 104, 120, 122, 128–129, 136

functionalist theory, 21

General Agreement of Tariffs and Trade (GATT), 48. *See also* World Trade Organization (WTO)

Giugni, Marco, 7

globacracies, 32, 36, 51, 93, 174n6 (chap. 2)

global bureaucratic institutions. *See* globacracies

globalization: cultural, 42–43; economic, 43–46; political, 46–50

global justice movement. *See* anti-globalization

globophobes/globofobicos, 156, 163

governmentality, 16, 25–26. *See also* Foucault, Michel

grounded theory, 38

Group of Eight (G8), 49–50. *See also* Group of Eight (G8) protests

Group of Eight (G8) protests, 72, 87–88, 94–95, 96, 101, 103, 139–140

Hardt, Michael, 16, 25, 27–31, 165, 167, 171, 174n3 (chap. 2)

Hayden, Tom, 111

Hobbes, Thomas, 19–20, 51

Houtart, François, 49

immaterial labor, 28–31, 174n3 (chap. 2)

Indymedia, 4–5, 63, 150

International Monetary Fund (IMF), 46–49. *See also* International Monetary Fund (IMF) protests

International Monetary Fund (IMF) protests: Washington (2002), 1–3, 9, 83; Washington (2000), 79–80, 160

King, Martin Luther, Jr., 6, 108, 134

King, Mike, 8

Kirchheimer, Otto, 10–11

Klein, Naomi, 151

Kraska, Peter, 100

labeling theory, 21–22

Locke, John, 19

Marcus, George, 39
Marx, Karl, 25, 27, 174n3
   (chap. 2)
McCarthy, John David, 13, 168
McHenry, Keith, 4
McPhail, Clark, 13–14, 81
meaning work, 139. *See also*
   frames
Miami model, 68
Mitchell, Don, 50, 93, 169
Morris, Aldon, 7
movement of movements, 51,
   173n1 (chap. 1). *See also* anti-
   globalization
Mueller, Carol, 7
multi-sited ethnography, 38–39
multitude, 16, 27–32

negotiated management model,
   12–15, 81–82, 145, 168–169
Negri, Antonio, 16, 25, 27–31
network-based movement, 17,
   92, 137
Nietzsche, Friedrich, 24

Pagan Cluster, 1–3, 45, 58
Park, Robert, 21
Parsons, Talcott, 21
People for the Ethical Treatment
   of Animals (PETA), 4–5
Polet, François, 49
police: corralling, 132; inducing
   fear of, 5, 76–77, 113, 149,
   153, 156; fortifying space,
   122–123; infiltration, 61,
   107–116; intelligence (data
   gathering), 102–116;
   intelligence operations,
   102–116; Miami, 68–69, 88,

97–105, 107, 110–111, 118,
   122–123, 128–131, 147–155;
   New York City, 73, 85,
   101–102, 120, 123–124, 132,
   162, 169; permits, 81–86;
   Public Affairs Communications
   Team (PACT), 141–147;
   reduce anonymity, 119–121;
   snatch squads (or extraction
   teams), 34, 133, 135–137,
   174n7 (chap. 2); targeted and
   mass preemptive arrests, 3, 65,
   133–137; Washington, D.C., 3,
   79–80, 90, 105, 120, 134–135,
   152, 155, 161
privatization, 44–45, 47
protest planning, 78, 81–82
protest sphere, 33

Ray, Raka, 33
repression: concept of, 8–9, 165;
   legal, 10–12, 90–91; soft, 10,
   77, 86. *See also* social control of
   dissent
repressive tactics: hard-line social
   control, 9, 15–16; soft-line
   social control; 9–10, 15–16
rhizome, 31, 174n5 (chap. 2)
Rousseau, Jean-Jacques, 19

securitization, 17, 161
security culture approach,
   113–116
September 11, 2001, 3–4,
   65–67, 174n7 (chap. 3), 175n2
   (chap. 4)
Shiller, Robert J., 48
Shiva, Vandana, 29, 44–45
Snow, David, 139, 156

social control: hard-line, 9,
15–16; overview, 19–23; soft-
line, 9–10, 14–16; social fields,
33; soft repression, 10. *See also*
social control of dissent
social control of dissent, 9, 14, 16,
23–24, 26, 32–33, 167, 173n3
spheres of control: legal, 32–33;
physical, 32, 34; psychological,
17, 32, 34
spokescouncil, 59–61
Starhawk, 2–3
Stiglitz, Joseph, 46–47
symbolic interactionism, 21

Tarrow, Sidney, 7
Tilly, Charles, 8

USA PATRIOT Act, 4, 66,
108–110, 175n3 (chap. 5)

Vahamaki, Jussi, 27
Vander Wall, Jim, 11
verstehen, 16, 38, 40, 173n5

Waddington, David, 7–8
Waddington, P.A.J., 13
Weber, Max, 40
World Economic Forum (WEF),
49, 51. *See also* World
Economic Forum (WEF)
protests
World Economic Forum (WEF)
protests, 73, 82, 123, 132,
168–169, 175n2 (chap. 4)
World Trade Organization
(WTO), 45, 48–49, 51, 167,
174n6 (chap. 2), 175n2
(chap. 4). *See also* World Trade
Organization (WTO) protests
World Trade Organization
(WTO) protests: Cancun
(2003), 46, 62, 94, 124, 175n2
(chap. 4), 176n6 (chap. 5);
Seattle (1999), 52, 56, 92–93,
122–123, 174n1; Qatar (2001),
94, 175n2 (chap. 4)

About the Author

Luis Fernandez, Jr., is an assistant professor in the criminal justice department at Northern Arizona University. He is a founding member of the Institute for the Study of Dissent and Social Control and is currently researching surveillance and its effects on dissent.